TOO MANY VOICES
My Journey from Confusion to Clarity

TOO MANY VOICES
My Journey from Confusion to Clarity

ALANE HAYNES

ETERNAL VOICE
PUBLISHING

Scripture quotations marked (AMPC) are taken from the Amplified Bible, Copyright © 1954, 1958, 1962, 1964, 1965, 1987 by The Lockman Foundation. Used by permission.

Scripture quotations marked (KJV) are taken from the Holy Bible, King James Version, Cambridge, 1769. Used by permission. All rights reserved.

Scripture quotations marked (NKJV) are taken from the New King James Version. Copyright © 1982 by Thomas Nelson, Inc. Used by permission. All rights reserved.

Emphasis of scripture quotations (italics, bold, etc.) have been added by the author for emphasis. Author has chosen not to capitalize satan or any reference to the devil.

Some names and identifying details have been changed to protect the privacy of individuals. I have written of events, locales and conversations from my memories of them. In order to maintain anonymity, in some instances, I may have changed the names of individuals and places, identifying characteristics and details such as physical properties, occupations and places of residence.

Any information in this book is not intended as a substitute for the medical advice of physicians. The reader should regularly consult a physician in matters relating to his/her health and particularly with respect to any symptoms that may require diagnosis or medical attention.

Published by Eternal Voice Publishing, San Diego, CA
Book design copyright © 2018 by Eternal Voice Publishing. All rights reserved.

ISBN-13:978-0692118146 (Eternal Voice Publishing)
ISBN-10: 0692118144

Cover and Logo Design by Justin Heinen
Editing, Layout & Interior Design by Cheryl Jenkins, *Kingdom One Business Solutions*

Published in the United States of America

Dedication

This book is dedicated to the Father, Son and Holy Spirit. Without the working of all three members of the Godhead in my life, I would still be in confusion and without hope.

Endorsements

In the pages of this book: *Too Many Voices*, Alane Haynes holds nothing back as she tells how the voice of strangers controlled her life early on. She is living proof that when God speaks, you live! When God speaks, you're healed! When God speaks, you're delivered! As you read her story, you will hear God's still small voice speaking into the broken places of your life and you will live again.

~ Bill Yount - Speaker and Author of: The Power of Real. www.billyount.com

"The New Covenant is one of transformation of the believer from Satan's image and power to God's. This author's story is a riveting testimony that serves as a battle flag of triumph flying at the top of the Adversary's mountain of darkness and discouragement. On the other side of Alane's overcoming by means of God's numerous personal interventions lies a victory of truth, deep life, and personal fulfillment on a scale of unimaginable proportions. She demonstrates first hand that life in our God can be complete, fulfilling and battle tested. A must read for those who are serious about discovering their destiny as God has shaped and designed it."

~ Rev. Earl Clampett: Simple Truth Ministries

Too Many Voices is a moving testimony of how God's plan, purpose and redemption can take one from a life full of confusion and destruction to a life full of purpose, hope and freedom. Alane's story will inspire you to trust in the goodness and promises of God no matter what you are going through. Alane has an amazing gift of sharing the truth about God and His character through the interpretations of her dreams and revelations. She will also encourage you and give you hope and victory through knowing how to declare the Living Word of God.

~ Karen Stevens - Pastor of Women's Ministries, Rock Church, San Diego, CA

Alane's book, *Too Many Voices*, is both transparent and authentic; from the very beginning she draws in her readers with the rawness of her story. This book is a powerful tool that can lead to personal growth, as it sheds light and revelation on the complex behavior patterns and coping mechanisms that people often gravitate towards after experiencing trauma and abuse. Alane boldly shares her story, even as far as going to the hard places that, frankly, many of us are unwilling to acknowledge due to fear. I highly recommend "Too Many Voices" to anyone, as I believe that this book will bring healing and freedom to many. The transformation that the Lord has done in Alane's life is truly remarkable. Her testimony makes known the faithfulness of the Lord, even down to the generations (Psalm 89:1). If you desire true freedom and healing, then this book is for you!

~ Angie Stolba - Author of: Dealing with the Root of Rejection;
writer for Elijah List and Spirit Fuel

In second Corinthians, scripture says that each of us is an epistle known and read by all men. As I read through Alane Haynes' book entitled *Too Many Voices*, I became aware that many of her self-proclaimed fears and apprehensions about not being good enough and seeking approval from others, were etched upon the pages of my own epistle, as well. I could tell that her journey - from listening and catering to the lying voices of doubt, despair, and depression to discovering and clinging to the one true and eternal voice of her Savior - is a journey that God wants all of us to make in one way or another. Her nuggets gleaned from Scripture, Holy Spirit intervention, and life's experiences should act as a balm of healing for all believers. But the biggest take away from her writing, was not how the Lord can heal me from buying into the many false voices in my own life, but how God has called each of us to be His voice to others.

~ Caz Taylor - "KPRZ Radio's Come Together San Diego" radio host,
Bible teacher, author, videographer

With a world filled with so many clamoring voices, one can so easily find themselves immersed in a fog of confusion. The voices of rejection and condemnation of past or present wounds try to hold you down. Alane Haynes book, *Too Many Voices - My Journey from Confusion to Clarity,* takes you on a powerful journey to find that One voice of clarity, the voice of your Beloved King. It is a powerful journey of pressing through the pain, overcoming all odds and soaring in the healing and glory of your King. I have to share my first thought as I began reading was simply "Wow! Praise God for his marvelous love and light that pierces through the darkness, through the fog and makes our paths clear. That one voice that in an instant brings hope, healing, and clarity!" God's love is fierce and relentless! You will find it expressed throughout this must have book!

~ Dana Jarvis - Evangelist and Author, Prophetic Seer, Founder of Hezekiah's Wall Ministry

Alane Haynes is a friend of mine and a beloved friend of God's! I want to say, "Thank You Alane for your open, honest and transparent heart!" *Too Many Voices* invites us to enter Alane's dark and painful past and examine our own story. We are taken on a life's journey of revival through forgiveness, healing, and restoration. This powerful story brings about the reality of transformation and eternal love that develops our true identity with the Eternal One.

The first poem, *Too Many Voices,* introduces the beautiful poetry which continues throughout the book resonating hope and healing!

Alane has listened well and heard the One True Voice loud and clear! *Too Many Voices* is a must read for all who have heard, listened and reacted to the voices of the world and the enemy. Alane Haynes invites us to silence those voices and become empowered with a new voice that resonates our true identity found in the Great I Am.

~ Lynda Miller - Founder and Pastoral Counselor of New Beginnings, Counseling Services, Carlsbad, CA

I have served alongside Alane in women's ministry for many years now, have read all of her books and knew that she was a gifted writer. But this particular book was different. There were many sections in the book *Too Many Voices* that touched me; there were days when I could not put this book down, it was so good! Also, the beautiful and heartfelt poems are priceless. Jesus has given Alane a platform to speak and connect with folks struggling with a lack of faith, low self-esteem and mental health challenges. She is speaking TRUTH into lives that truly matter to our Abba Father, the Savior of the world! His plans for Alane were all laid out, years and years in advance; He never gave up on her. This book clearly shows how God is always chasing after us with "Reckless Abandon." There are people out there who have lost all hope. Alane is a "HOPE DEALER," an Ambassador for Christ.

~ Lisa Thrift-Blatnica — Pastor, Rock Church San Diego, Disaster Chaplain & "The Coaching Chaplain" thecoachingchaplain.com

I was delighted to be invited by Alane Haynes to write an endorsement for her new book: *Too Many Voices — My Journey from Confusion to Clarity*. Alane's wonderful book details the clash of the kingdom of sin, pain, addiction and abuse met head on by the Kingdom of God when Jesus wrests the soul of the tormented from the grip of evil. Alane's gritty story of her journey from the depths of despair and gloomy 'forecasts' give way to the clear blue skies of freedom and joy that is on offer through Jesus. Her Christ-centered bio will help you weed out the confusing voices in your own life that are competing for your destiny and help you enjoy the fair winds and following seas that God so graciously provides to those who respond to His invitation. Most everyone enjoys a roller coaster ride...that's what you'll find within these pages: ups and downs, quick turns and concerns and a big finish that leaves you looking back thinking, WOW, we made it!

~ Kevin Sanford — Pastor, The Mission Church, Poway, CA

Alane Haynes book, *Too Many Voices,* is a must read for anyone wanting to break through the myriads of voices from our past into embracing the new voice of victory! Her life story will impact and strike your heart. Lean into the pages of this story and you'll find the voice of a loving, faithful Father ready to heal you now!

~ Maria Sainz - Co-founder and Senior pastor, Red Seal Ministries

I really enjoyed the book *Too Many Voices* by Alane Haynes. I thought I was just going to help out a friend, and I was very surprised when I found that this book was for me! It spoke to me personally. We all hear voices in our head, and it is a problem trying to figure out which are God's, which are ours, and which are the enemy's. This book helps us do that. *Too Many Voices* is a book for everyone, whether non-Christians or Christians, young in faith or mature. It took a lot of courage for Alane to put her story on paper. Her writing is refreshingly transparent and honest, and her story is interspersed with very good poetry. I *really* liked this book; it is one of the best books I have ever read!

~ Wayne Clarke - Senior Pastor, His Dwelling Place Ministries

Alane Haynes book *Too Many Voices* is one of great trials and great triumphs. This is an inspiring and timely book for this generation. As she draws the reader in with her childhood testimony and the breakdown of the strongholds in her generations we are shown that nothing is impossible with God. Alane is the living embodiment of the verse in Revelation 12:11 that declares we overcome Satan by the Blood of the Lamb and the word of our testimony. Alane's story shows us that the battle on earth is real but that we can overcome with Him who has called us to life and victory. Her love for Jesus permeates the pages and her passion for His Kingdom to be advanced inspires the reader to want to do the same! I also strongly encourage anyone who has suffered from victimization and mental health issues to read this book.

~ Jill Shankles - Counselor and Founder of Armor of Light Breakthrough Ministries

In *Too Many Voices - My Journey from Confusion to Clarity*, Alane shares, with great vulnerability, her life story amid brokenness and pain. For those struggling with childhood traumas and tormenting thoughts, her transparency and journey towards freedom in Christ will encourage you and provide some helpful insights in your own healing.

~ Wanda Alger - Writer for Intercessors for America, prophetic minister, and author of three books including, "*Oracles of Grace: Building a Legacy of Wisdom and Revelation.*"

Acknowledgements

To my two beautiful daughters, Cara and Sara. I am so thankful to God for both of you. I have to say that there were times in my life that the two of you were the only reason I had for living. I am so proud of the women you have become. I am forever grateful to God for your being in my life, but also to the both of you for your love for me when I wasn't the best. I cherish the deep relationship we have. And now you have given me grandchildren! I am so blessed!

To my husband Kerry, I am so thankful that God brought us together. Your belief in me, reminding me of who I am when I forget, and your unfailing support of my calling, is one of the best gifts I have ever received. I love what God is doing through us together as heirs together of the grace of Life!

To my siblings and other relatives, your continual love and prayers, especially when my life was in turmoil, provided a foundation that I was unaware of at the time but thankful for now.

A special thank you to my brother David, for editing the first draft of my manuscript. I appreciate your discernment and value your expertise. I know that it probably wasn't easy re-living some family memories.

A special thank you to my son-in-law Justin Heinen, for patiently enduring my quest for the perfect logo and book cover design! Your creativity and skill is amazing.

To Billie Alexander and all my spiritual family at Limitless Realms International Ministries, thank you! I have grown so much in my gifts and calling through the rich atmosphere of the Holy Spirit whenever we gather, the apostolic alignment and prophetic release, and for the undergirding of what God is doing in our lives.

To Karen Stevens and Lisa Thrift-Blatnica at the Rock Church, I am thankful for the opportunities given in ministry, and for your friendship and support on my journey.

To my friends, and to my co-laborers in the Kingdom of God, thank you for adding to my life. What you carry within you has brought blessing and increase of eternal value.

Too Many Voices

Too many voices
Robbing my peace,
Crowding the one voice
That brings my release.

The voices of fear,
Doubt and worry,
The voice that says, "Much to do,
Better hurry, hurry, hurry."

The voice that listens
For the approval of man
That clouds the clarity
Of knowing God's plan.

The voice that says
My voice doesn't matter;
The voice that desires to fill silence
With chatter.

Yet there is only One voice I desire to hear,
The only voice that is crystal clear.
For when it all is said and done,
I seek the highest prize that can be won -
To see the Kingdom of God
Manifest through His Son.

Table of Contents

Foreword

I have had the honor of knowing Alane Haynes since 2012. Alane and her husband, Kerry, are regional ministers aligned with Limitless Realms International Ministries and also are involved in the corporate expression of worship throughout San Diego, California and beyond.

Alane is a skilled apostolic teacher, Kingdom prophet and a gifted writer. As you read Alane's new book, *Too Many Voices - My Journey from Confusion to Clarity*, many of you will be blessed as you move with Alane on her journey. The definition of journey is a long and often difficult process of personal change and development. Alane is very transparent and forthright as she shares her struggles but also the overcoming victories that have been used to conform her into the image of her King as well as an established minister of the gospel.

Too Many Voices will aid the reader to recognize the Voice in the midst of the many voices. Isaiah 11:2 speaks prophetically of the coming Messiah where the Spirit of the Lord will rest upon Him, the Spirit of wisdom and understanding, the Spirit of counsel and might, and the Spirit of knowledge and the fear of the Lord. Because Alane has learned to abide in the Lord Jesus Christ and has received the mind of Christ; that same Spirit that rested upon Jesus also rests upon Alane. Her relationship with Jesus will encourage the reader not to give up but will impart the critical understanding to this profound and much needed truth for the Body of Christ: With the purpose of bringing forth Godly inheritance, we must be willing to persevere in faith, appropriate the revealed truth of the Word, and to walk in the Spirit of Grace and Holiness.

I admire my friend Alane, as she has proven time and time again that she is more than a conqueror, releasing this life changing principle throughout this book.

Billie E. Alexander
Director / Co-Founder
Limitless Realms International Ministries, Inc., San Diego, California

Preface

I was given the mandate to write this book shortly after my first book, "Moses – Shocked in the Desert, Learning God's Ways So We Can Enter the Promised Land," was published in 2014. I knew that it was to be my story, the many testimonies of Jesus Christ in my life, and clearly heard Holy Spirit whisper the title to me: *"Too Many Voices – My Journey from Confusion to Clarity."*

Upon starting this book, there came a sudden attack on my mind. Ironically, I could not identify the voices; it was as if a heavy fog rolled in rendering me mentally paralyzed. In fact, I was very angry and didn't want to write the book. Looking back, I can see that the struggle began after I started writing about some of the childhood trauma I experienced and I became fearful of hurting my mother, who was still alive, or damaging the memory of my father, or harming my siblings or others in my life.

A short time later, I had a dream that I was in a house with two bathrooms, and I had a baby I needed to set somewhere safe. The only safe place seemed to be the bathtub, as it had high sides. However, my mother was running water for her bath in one of them. Somehow the two bathtubs were connected. The water in my mother's tub was filling mine and I was trying to find a way to stop her water from running into my tub. I didn't know what to do, as I didn't want to disturb my mother's bathwater, but I didn't want my baby to drown. Wow. Talk about profound.

There was an obvious conflict in my subconscious, and there is a war in the Kingdom. There was fear to share some of my experience because I loved my mother and didn't want to hurt her, yet this book was my baby and I had to find a safe place to share it without fear of it being drowned. The truth is that I know I have said and done things that harmed my children, and I didn't do it intentionally. I love my mother and know that she didn't harm me intentionally, nor did my father or siblings or anyone else. Yet I also know that there is power in the truth, and freedom comes with truth. So here I go. The enemy will be cast down and those generational iniquities in our bloodline will cease. Others will read and light will shine in the darkness for them and their generations will be freed also. Father God, Thine is the Kingdom and the Glory and the Power, forever. Amen.

Introduction

"There are, it may be, so many kinds of voices in the world, and none of them is without signification."   I Corinthians 14:10 (KJV)

This book is written with intent, to bring hope and faith in situations that seem hopeless.

If you are a parent or grandparent, I hope that this book will encourage and exhort you to speak words of life into your children. Let my story show you the powerful effects of words, both positive and negative.

If you are struggling with a difficult journey, especially those who are confused and don't know if there is a way out of the darkness, I pray that my book will bring hope and healing to you. If you do not know the Lord, or are not even sure if there is a God, please keep reading. You may identify with some of my journey and find light for yours.

If you are a person who "sees" or "hears" or "senses" things in another realm, and have thought you are crazy, or been told you are crazy, I hope this book will bring enlightenment, alignment to the true purpose of your gifts, and courage to know and fulfill your purpose.

I pray that you will receive faith after seeing what God has done in my life, and begin to believe that He can do it for you, and/or for those you in your life who may be struggling. He is not a respecter of persons. If God did it for me, He will do it for you (Romans 2:13).

It can be a long journey, but it is worth it. There is nothing that compares to peace of mind, knowing beyond a shadow of a doubt that He will lead you into the way everlasting and that you will know it is His voice you are hearing. His word is sharp and powerful, piercing even to the dividing asunder of soul and spirit (Hebrews 4:12). Your spirit will receive His words of life and grow, and send healing into your soul.

The purpose of telling my story is to bring hope to those who may find themselves stuck in one of the places on my journey, to shine a light on the path and make the way a little clearer and easier to navigate, and to bring glory to God for His faithfulness and goodness and mercy in my life. I thank God that He brought me on this path and, at times, carried me, led me or pushed me. There were times He literally plucked me out and set me in another place. I hold no grudges, have no unforgiveness, to any who wronged me, whether intentionally or not. I believe most people do not purposefully inflict harm on others, but act out of their own brokenness, whether realized or not. We live in a fallen world and are all broken and in need of a Savior and Healer.

Before I start telling the story of my journey from confusion to clarity, I want to say that I *love* my family and have many good memories of enjoyable times as a child — memories of great times together laughing, playing games, just doing the normal things of life together. My Mom and Dad were human and did the best they could with the knowledge they had and the reality of who they are in their personalities and gifts. Truly, a family can be a microcosm of the Body of Christ, a place where individual members with unique gifts have to learn to love one another, be a safe haven to work out their salvation in fear and trembling. Unfortunately, most people do not have that awareness and even if they did, part of the process of growth and healing is that those closest to us sometimes bring out the worst in ourselves before we have a chance to collect our thoughts and react "right."

I bare my soul to you, the reader, in full awareness that you may judge me for some of the things I did in my life. I hope and pray that you will see the patterns and choices I made that led to my mistakes so that you can learn from them and choose wisely yourself. I often had to learn the hard way, but God is faithful, the ultimate teacher. He is patient and kind, yet also disciplines in order to keep us going in the right direction, praise be to His Holy Name!

After the Lord gave me the title for this book, I began to search out the scriptures that talked about confusion.

> *"Woe to the rebellious children, saith the LORD, that take counsel, but not of me; and that cover with a covering, but*

not of my spirit, that they may add sin to sin: That walk to go down into Egypt, and have not asked at my mouth; to strengthen themselves in the strength of Pharaoh, and to trust in the shadow of Egypt! Therefore shall the strength of Pharaoh be your shame, and the trust in the shadow of Egypt your confusion." Isaiah 30:1-3 (KJV)

"We lie down in our shame, and our confusion covereth us: for we have sinned against the LORD our God, we and our fathers, from our youth even unto this day, and have not obeyed the voice of the LORD our God." Jeremiah 3:25 (KJV)

These verses were eye-opening to me. We sin and turn to our own counsel. For a child that was abused, this is hard to receive, because the pain and wounds are inflicted by another. Yet when I look back, I can see that as a child there was a shutting down that occurred because of abuse (mental, emotional, sexual) but not the confusion of too many voices. That came later.

My journey into confusion began with open doors to the enemy created by wounds. Through those doors, many voices came in causing doubt, rebellion, conflict and emotional/mental paralysis, leading to my graver sins and causing more wounds to myself and others. My journey out of confusion and into clarity was very difficult and painful, but worth every moment of every struggle and battle. I now have peace. I have learned to identify and silence voices that steal joy, kill peace and destroy sanity. I know the voice of God. Jesus said, "My sheep hear my voice, and I know them, and they follow me." John 10:27 (KJV)

Learning to trust God, to make Jesus Lord of all of my life, took a lot longer than the initial receiving Him into my heart and trusting Him as Savior and Healer.

This is a book of my painful and difficult journey of growth, born from the desire to have change in my life, dissatisfaction with the recurring pains and loss and the knowledge that there was something better. This is not a book of retelling funny, cute, happy times. I had those too, and I thank God for them. Those, perhaps, were what kept me from developing a complete hardness of heart. There are times, you will see, that I forgot the vision of hope and did give myself over to bitterness for a season, but God continued to work with me faithfully, patiently drawing me back to Him and to His purpose for my life.

In His Heart

Mine is a love story, older than time.
Seen through the lens of His hand taking mine
Leading me gently back to the start
Before time began, I existed in His heart.

It is a story of discovery — discovery that the Maker of all things has loved me with an everlasting love; before time began I was with Him, in Christ Jesus, and at the pre-appointed time He sent me forth with a destiny imprinted within me that would require forging in the furnace of affliction, allowing the enemy to harm me...to a point...in those very areas where God would later come in, with Power, Light, and Love. For in those areas, those wounds, that is where His power will come forth to lead others into their destiny in Christ.

Truly, the journey is one of returning, to come back to the First Voice, the Voice of the Beloved calling us to Himself.

As long as we draw breath upon this earth, God is always waiting for us to turn to Him. His promises are *yea* and *amen,* He promises that if we return to Him with our whole heart, He will heal us and restore us. (Joel 2:12-27; Zechariah 9:12; Deuteronomy 30) We see this not only in the Old Testament, but the entire New Testament speaks of restoration when we turn to the Lord with all of our heart. That is my story.

Double for Your Trouble

The enemy came to bring you trouble
I say, for your shame you shall have double
The enemy's plans are overturned
You were seen as a woman spurned
But now I have set you in a high place
With a double portion of my grace
The enemy is defeated, bound
Your testimony has produced a sound
In it, freedom for others is found

A Helpful Tool

I thought it might be helpful to share with you the type of analysis I applied in regard to identifying the voices, defeating the lies and walking in the Truth, which brings clarity. This is what I had to do to make the corrections along the course of my journey, to see what (or who) I was listening to. The different voices needed to be identified, and the source, or root, of them.

I share this to offer a tool that you can use if, when reading my story, you begin to question if perhaps some of the situations in your life might be occurring because of the voices you are listening to, and you too, begin to desire change. I am praying that the Spirit of Truth will pierce every area of darkness and clarity will come, leading to a life of love, joy and peace in the Holy Ghost.

> *Perception is the filter of our experiences.*

Our reality is, in part, skewed by our interpretation of events as we remember them. The Bible says, *"As a man thinketh in his heart, so is he."* Proverbs 23:7 (KJV) My view of my childhood and young adult life has changed over the years.

I have found that our focus in life, and the manifestation we experience, is largely based on the voices we are listening to (including our own), how we interpret those voices through our internal filters/beliefs, and the conclusions we draw from them. The reason I feel a need to emphasize this is because in telling the journey from confusion to clarity, I will have to tell you how confusion came in, what were the seeds that were sown in the ground of my heart that would later manifest on the road named choice.

I can remember as a child of ten or so being in the library. I was bored of my books, so I was wandering the aisles when a book caught my eye. It was a psychology textbook, filled with intriguing thought-provoking questions to ask patients such as, "Did you have a happy childhood?" Such a basic question, yet it astonished and puzzled me. What is happiness? What would a "happy childhood" look like? It would be many more years before I would begin to notice the difference in families and how they function. I had rarely been to other friend's homes and, truly, unless you spend a lot of time in another's home, you don't get a true picture of the relationships. Adults tend to be on "good" behavior when others are there.

The Bible says to train up a child in the way he should go, and when he is old he will not depart from it (Proverbs 22:6). It is so true, but not in the way I think most interpret it. I think most people think that we "train" our children by what we tell them, but in reality much of their training is by watching others and perceiving what is not spoken. It is very confusing for a child to hear his or her parents telling them to do one thing but seeing them do something else.

I learned in a Behavioral Science class that our mind categorizes everything and when things happen, we immediately put it in one of those categories, or boxes. In other words, we subconsciously think, "Oh, this is like the time that..." and then make judgments about it based on our earlier experiences. These internal "voices" cause us to respond automatically in situations that have similarities to earlier ones. Yet, as adults, we would be better served by our experiences if we set our thoughts aside momentarily and asked God, "What do You have to say about this situation?" The Bible says if we ask God for wisdom, He will give it abundantly (James 1:5). Many of our problems exist because we aren't listening or seeing things as they truly are, we've already drawn our conclusions.

For instance, if you experience a deep rejection as a child, it is likely that in every situation where there is anything remotely resembling the earlier instance, whether it be facial expression, tone of voice, body language, etc., you will feel rejected because you automatically categorized it as such and responded that way. My experience has been that God sets us up with future experiences so that we have opportunities to be healed. When you begin to hear the voice of rejection, when you feel those feelings, you may ask God to help you and He will. He is your comforter, the friend who sticks closer than a brother (Proverbs 18:24).

There comes a time when we realize that there is a "voice" of rejection, a "spirit" of rejection that has come to live with us and we are hearing its voice. If you are saved by the Lord Jesus Christ, you have His Spirit – the Holy Spirit – abiding in you. The Holy Spirit is the Spirit of Truth. Therefore, any other voices that contradict His Truth are not of God. Whether it is your memory, or another spirit, or the internal voice giving you reasons justifying why you think things are the way you perceive them to be, those other voices lie. You may have been rejected once, but that doesn't mean that every person in a situation resembling the earlier time is rejecting you.

There is an unseen reality, a spiritual reality. Some may think it's all in the mind and I have thought that myself in the past. Then there came a time when I was feeling greatly oppressed and my "positive thinking" wasn't working anymore. I was desperate and decided to try out things I'd seen and heard others do. I said out loud, "Get off me, spirit of rejection; every unclean spirit leave me now in the name of Jesus. I am under the covering of His blood that was shed for me." Subsequently, I felt a shift in the atmosphere. The voices, torment and oppression stopped. Some may think I was just refusing those thoughts. Either way, the voices were stilled. In other words, it worked. In many ways, I have become a pragmatist. I find out what works and do it.

So this is what I do when I am confused or in a negative place:

1. Identify the words I am hearing. Sometimes this is the hardest part. I can remember times when I was hearing so many voices it seemed my mind was a jumble of hamsters in cages racing on their wheels, just a cacophony of confusion. At times I would throw myself on the bed and force myself to lay there until the voices would expend themselves and I could finally focus on one thing. There were two times in my backsliding years where I had to go on Prozac to quiet my mind while I developed coping tools for what was happening in my life. If you need professional help, if the darkness is too much and overwhelming, do what you need to do! Seek professional help.
2. Can I identify whose voice is it? My mother, father, self-condemnation, vague sense of "something wrong" or other negative feeling? Holy Spirit is always clear and to the point, very specific in one area needing correction. The enemy of our souls brings

condemnation, a very vague and underlying sense of something wrong with you, doom and gloom, hopelessness and emptiness.

3. Is it recurring?
    a. If so, was there a core belief formed from it, such as "No one will ever love me, I am damaged goods," "I am worthless," "My life will never be good," etc.
    b. Can I identify when and where it started?
    c. Is it a lie? In other words, what does God say about it? (If you aren't a Christian or don't believe in God, perhaps you have awareness that there is a different, better way to think and desire to be more positive or self-accepting. Keep going, please.)

4. Is it from an obvious wound? If you were abandoned, abused, rejected, cheated...those are obvious wounds.
    a. Ask for healing. (I pray that my story of healing will bring hope and faith that you can be healed.)

5. If not from a wound, recognize the voice might be a lie (recognizing the truth from what God says; if you aren't a believer, you can see it is a lie because it isn't resulting in what you thought it would and the result is pain, addiction, sickness, broken relationships, etc.).

6. What is the "hook" that caused me to believe the lie? Some examples —a reasoning that justified a wrong choice; a result that seemed pleasing to my eyes, or my flesh, or something that brought temporary satisfaction to an area of lack or need in my life...an easy, short-lived "fix." These are some of the "hooks" that cause us to believe a lie and become deceived.

7. Ask for wisdom and truth, clarity and healing. When you find Truth, stand on it and believe it above all the other voices. Refuse to back down from Truth.

The Early Years

(The Good, the Bad and the Ugly)

Family Formations

I was the middle child of five, with a pretty large gap in between the older two and younger two, so for all intents and purposes, I felt like an only child. I loved my parents and siblings, in the way that kids love. There was a lot of loneliness in my childhood, although the general feeling in our house was confusion and chaos from so many kids. There was also confusion because the things we were taught about right and wrong didn't line up with the behaviors that were exhibited, as well as words that were spoken that weren't congruent with the spirit in which they were expressed.

My oldest sister Joy and I shared a room at times, but I didn't really get to know her well until I was an adult. As a child, I was closest to brother, David, even though he was seven years older than me. He was usually the one who played with me. Granted, a lot of it was teasing and horseplay, but I always knew he loved me. When he went away to ROTC in Georgia, and graduate school in Pennsylvania, I was devastated. It was right around the time that boys became important. I have often wondered if some of my choices were because of the emptiness I felt after he left home. My younger sisters Bonnie and Mindy were kids I had to watch, for the most part, until I became older. We are all very close now.

My Dad loved the Lord deeply. God revealed His calling as a preacher to my dad when he almost died from a bone infection in the ear. My Mom also loved the Lord. She was raised by godly parents who lived out their faith in the home. Yet with both my parents, there were wounds in their souls that led to character defects and communication breakdowns, walls erected that kept intimacy from developing, great fears that kept them bound and family dynamics formed that were very unhealthy.

We all know that if bacteria enters a wound, infection is likely to follow. In the spiritual, it is the same. We receive a wound in our soul – a profound hurt or disappointment or loss, a betrayal or misunderstanding - and the enemy is ready and waiting to infect us with his lies. "See, they don't care, they don't really love you;" "God doesn't care about you, where was He when you needed Him?" An infected wound in our physical body becomes very painful to touch. We do everything we can to avoid touching that spot, it hurts terribly. Yet at some point it must be addressed. The infection has to be cleaned out so that it can heal. In the same way, if we do not deal with our emotional wound(s), we become stuck in time emotionally and towards God. We erect walls around that wound so that no one can touch it and expose that great pain. Bitterness and unforgiveness form, and we give the enemy access to our heart.

As a child, putting up walls to protect from further wounds is a great protective mechanism. Sometimes the painful events are too much for a child's psyche, if there is no one around to help the child work through it, a trusted adult who is healthy enough to provide the love and acceptance that is needed. In those cases, when the trauma is too great, and the very ones that wounded them are those who are responsible for their well-being, then the child turns inward and hides his or her core being, eventually creating a false identity that is accepted by those in charge. It is amazing to me how early one can develop this survival mode, so early that we actually come to believe that false persona is who we are. You will see how my false identity formed as you read my story.

A large part of my childhood life revolved around church. My dad sequestered himself in the study to work on sermons for Sunday. He went visiting the sick and those needing prayer. He was involved in different service organizations and would often be called upon to be a speaker. Besides being a music teacher at the public school, my mom was very involved in the church as the Pastor's wife. She often, and at varied times, filled multiple roles of organist, choir director, Sunday school teacher, Women's Ministry leader, etc.

At the time I grew up, and in the small towns where we lived, there very few activities for youth after school; not that my parents would have been able to afford it or transport us, with five kids, one car, and not a lot of extra money. My memories of childhood were playing outside, reading books, or getting harassed and teased by my older siblings who (it seemed to me) alternated between loving me and resenting having to watch me. Saturdays my mom would clean, do laundry, bake for the week and go shopping. We kids would have a share in some of those activities. Sundays were church, a large meal after church with an occasional visit from an elder or visiting Bishop, and my Dad and brother watching sports on TV.

I believe that much of the conflict in our home occurred because my parents were so different in their gifts, callings, and personalities. Later in life, as I became more cognizant of the gifts that God gives and how they interact with each other, it was apparent to me why there was so much frustration between my parents.

My dad was a United Methodist minister, and I am thankful for the requirement to go to Sunday School and church every week, because I know now that there were many seeds of the Word of God planted in my soul. I loved the songs sung in church, the stained glass windows, and the feeling of the sacred and divine, the reverence and repetition of prayers and creeds. I know that there were deep foundational beliefs laid from these things, as there were times in my life that I could only go "so far" even though I would not understand why.

My dad was a gifted preacher and teacher. I believe he was gifted as a prophet but it was stifled by religion. My understanding is that most churches during that time didn't embrace the gifts of apostle or prophet. It was believed, generally, that those gifts were not for today. In fact, none of the gifts were emphasized. It was more about being a moral person and following rules and traditions. My dad struggled greatly with temptation and was frustrated and moody because of his dual nature. He was expressive and full of life and joy when he was in a good mood. He was highly disciplined, very intense and focused. He could be very acerbic and say things that would cut deeply. When he failed in his disciplines, he would punish himself. When he would say things that he regretted, he would put masking tape on his mouth to remind himself to control his tongue.

My mother was also a gifted teacher. She loved music and was an excellent pianist and singer. Both of my parents had beautiful voices and loved the hymns. My mother was a music teacher and enjoyed teaching children piano as well. Her gifts included mercy and helping others. She had a strong love of family and was aware later in life that her love of family actually hindered the work of the Holy Spirit at times, as her "helping" would sometimes cause her to interfere with the processes of God in others' lives. It is a danger to all of us, especially moms, as we long to "help" those we love. She would try and minimize the harmful things my father said in his bad moods by singing or being silly with us, and she was great at distracting us with activities. "Keeping busy" was a tool she relied on often. I can remember her saying, "Idle hands are the devil's workshop." My mother disliked emotional expression; she did not trust emotions and was careful not to be led by them.

Although my parents were Christians, and my father a minister of the Gospel, the Word was never spoken in our house and the only prayers I heard in my home as a child were rote dinner prayers. There was a lot of dysfunction and an atmosphere of sexual deviance in my family, all covered up and emotions suppressed. It actually was not until much later in my life that I found out a lot of what was happening.

One of the things I found out was that my dad was a cross-dresser and enjoyed pornography. He was accused of molesting two of my sisters and two grandsons. He denied this, but admitted to the cross-dressing. He didn't think it was harming anyone. When I questioned my dad about his cross-dressing later in life (I was in my 50's) he told me that he thought most women didn't "dress up" that well, and that he could do it better. My grandmother was a very well dressed woman. She always wore jewelry, makeup and fixed her hair. She wore hats, hose, and high heels. I never saw her casually dressed.

I have a vague memory of seeing my dad dressed up with makeup on and wondering why this strange woman was in our house. There was also a time, when snooping in my father's dresser, finding a woman's black brassiere and underwear, wondering why my mom's clothes were in his dresser drawers. This also makes me wonder what else may have been going on in my grandparents' house, if there were some perversity leading to my father's sinful predisposition.

The family story is that my father's mother had some type of mental illness. She was certainly unique in personality – very outspoken and opinionated. She did love the Word of God, though. She gave me money to memorize Bible verses. I remember memorizing the fruit of the Spirit and receiving $1.00, which was a lot of money in the early 60's. My grandparents were very frugal, having gone through the Great Depression, and feared not having money. She and my grandfather didn't trust banks; they hid money all over their house.

My grandmother had many different "careers" in her life. One of her later careers was as a nurse, and she often had many pill bottles lying around, enough to certainly question if there were substance abuse (not that it was a topic in those days). I'm certain that some of her behavior was due to the assortment of pills she was taking. I have thought that my grandmother may have been the source of my dad being a cross-dresser, as I remember pictures of him as a baby and young child in feminine attire. I also know that she wanted a little girl. She had a still-born baby girl that would have been my dad's younger sister.

My grandmother was very jealous of my mother's relatives. Once she told me that she knew I loved her more because she gave me money. That wasn't true, but it made me feel torn as if I had to choose. There was a lot of that in my family. There seemed to be an underlying competition between my dad and my brother for the attention of the other family members. My dad, being an only child, was used to having a lot of attention and perhaps he felt my brother was taking some of what he was due.

I used to have two recurring nightmares that are related to this dynamic. In one, I was on a checkerboard in outer space that was rotating very fast. I was being chased by Captain Kangaroo and Mr. Greenjeans. I always woke up before I was caught, shaking and in a sweat. The second nightmare was that I was in hell, on one side of a deep chasm with flames shooting up from the chasm. The devil was standing with me. My whole family was on the other side. The devil told me that I would have to choose one person to be saved. The others would go into the pit of fire. I woke up petrified, sweating and shaking each time I had that nightmare.

My dad's father was very quiet and gruff, and I didn't have any type of relationship with him at all. My impression of him was that he did not like children. I often heard him saying that children should be "seen and not heard." When we visited them, the kids ate first and then the adults. My oldest sister recently revealed that when she was little our grandfather spent a lot of time with her, even taking her to the movies. One summer that ended. She has memories of molestation and thinks it might have been him; it would certainly explain why none of us were ever alone with him again.

My mom experienced great trauma as a child. She was the oldest of four children - two girls and two boys - and she said her parents were wonderful, kind Christians. They were poor, living in the Dust Bowl of Oklahoma in a converted boxcar (her father worked for the railroad). However, they never lacked food and were generous to hobos that came via the railroad looking for help. My mother's mother died when my mom was six years old and my mom became the "little mom" to her younger siblings. When she was 10, she was sent to live with a preacher and his family for the summer to help them out as they had just had a baby, and had two other children. During her time there she was molested by the preacher. I did not know that until the last year of my mother's life when she shared that with me. I may have been the first person she shared that with. It is such a blessing to me that my relationship with my mother was transformed in her later years so that I could truly honor her before she passed into eternity.

My mother's dad remarried when my mom was around 10, and he died when she was 13. The stepmother didn't feel she could handle the girls and sent them to live with my mother's Aunt Olive in Washington, D.C. My mom and her sister didn't see their brothers for eight years. So I came to understand at a much later age that my mom's coping mechanism was to stay busy and not feel things, as she had to do that when her mother died, and then her father. I know that she did not have an outlet for her feelings, nor was there anyone to help her with them.

Of course, as a child I didn't know that. I felt she didn't understand me or love me. Once I had two children our relationship changed; that was one area where we could relate. I could see in her eyes that she recognized my difficulty in coping with the demands of two small children so close in age, and that awareness provided needed support when she came to visit, even though we didn't talk about it at that time.

Aunt Olive (Momaw) and her husband Dan (Bopaw) were the most wonderful people I knew as a child. They made me feel so special and loved. They were truly grandparents to me, and I am so thankful for them. Bopaw Dan died of complications of diabetes when I was eight; I was devastated and heartbroken. He was so kind and loving, as was Momaw.

Momaw nurtured my love of nature; she had the most beautiful yard full of flowers and shrubs she had planted, and she fed the birds and squirrels daily.

Momaw always took time to answer my questions about nature and God. I remember asking her why the wind blew and where it came from. She said that God sends wind to bring breezes and clean the air.

When I came to visit, she would treat me like royalty. She would bring out the good china and serve me at the dining room table, which had a big picture window with a view of part of her yard. I could watch the birds landing in the birdbath, splashing and drinking. I hated leaving their house. I asked Momaw once if I could come and live with them. I remember her look of kindness and compassion. She said, "Laney, I would love that, but it would hurt your Momma so much."

I am so thankful for Momaw and Bopaw and their deep love and kindness. They planted seeds that would bear good fruit in the latter years of my life. Why am I telling you these things? I am giving you a little generational background to show, in part, why my parents were the way that they were. None of us have our lives completely unaffected from previous generations, and by examining the generations before we can learn about traits we have and where they come from. Does it matter? I think it does; at the least it brings a broader understanding and compassion for our parents and we can apply that compassion to others as well, learning that we all are broken and come from a line of broken individuals. For me, it makes me want to "end the madness" and forge new paths.

To be fair, our family had wonderful times together also. We had times of playing games together that were filled with laughter. We had family vacations where the "normal" activities ceased and there was good interaction among all of us, albeit challenging times also. My parents did the best they could with what they knew. We were provided for in the daily necessities of life and never went to bed hungry. Our parents insisted we go to church and we were taught to be considerate of and kind to others, respectful of all, to live in moderation and be good citizens. We just weren't close in the sense of sharing meaningful discussions or things that mattered to our hearts. After many painful family traumas, we have changed those dynamics now.

So now you have a snapshot view of my family. As you hear more, some of you will think I had a terrible childhood, others will think it was average, still others will think it was wonderful compared to theirs. As I get back to the telling of my journey, my intent is that you will see how God worked it all together for His plans and purposes (which are always good), and be able to re-examine your past in the light of His Glory. For these I now know are true:

> "And we know that all things work together for good to them that love God, to them who are the called according to his purpose." Romans 8:28 (KJV)

> "But as for you, ye thought evil against me; but God meant it unto good, to bring to pass, as it is this day, to save much people alive." Genesis 50:20 (KJV)

Filled with Glory

Though the pain and the tears
Have accompanied you many years
The wounds inflicted will become
The dwelling place of my Son
And the pain will be undone
Filled with my Glory, brighter than the sun
The battle has already been won
In time, with Him you will be one

Unseen Realities
("You're Crazy!")

A series of events that occurred in my childhood were very traumatic in the formation of my identity, so much so that I shut down and mentally left my body when confrontation occurred. I had heard and received the voice of shame in the depths of my being. When other instances arose where there was the slightest hint of confrontation, I shut down and had no thoughts. It was as if my mind became paralyzed and I was unable to respond. As I became older, if someone asked me a personal question or wanted my opinion about something, I would shut down mentally and emotionally, actually be completely blank in my mind, break out in a sweat and be nauseous for fear of saying the wrong thing and being told I was crazy.

As a child, I was very sensitive to the unspoken things. When I talked about how I felt or things I saw or experienced. I heard these reprovals: "You're crazy;" "That didn't happen;" "We are Christians, so you don't feel that" and so on. I felt shame and loneliness, fear that I was crazy, certainty that there was something wrong with me. These were some of the voices that kept me bound in fear. I learned not to trust my own thoughts and feelings and became an expert at discerning what others were thinking and feeling so I could mimic them and do the "right" thing. I yearned for acceptance. Although I was a very good student, getting mostly A's, somehow it was never enough.

Even in Sunday School, there were voices of mocking, reinforcing my belief that I was crazy. We were asked to draw a picture of heaven once, when I was about six years old. The teacher looked at my picture, smirked and said, "Heaven doesn't look like that! That looks like a birthday cake!!" Interestingly, when I became a Christian and read in the Book of Revelation the Apostle John's description of heaven, it looked like my picture! What I remember being in my mind's eye as I drew, was a beautiful castle positioned on streets of gold. The walls of the castle were shimmering and translucent, studded with jewels of every color.

I was so afraid of hurting others' feelings, losing their love, that I would make pretend I liked things I really didn't, to gain approval. Christmas and birthdays were horrifying for me, as I might receive a present I didn't like and hurt someone's feelings by not having the "right" response. I would practice ahead of time to make my face "just right." In fact, I became really good at finding presents that were hidden so I could know ahead of time and practice my face.

Truth Unspoken

If the words have not been said
Still remaining in their head
Are they less truth?
Does speech give proof?
To one with the gift of a tuned-in ear
Or the one who has visions, known as a seer,
The reality they sense
Is very clear.
Yet to those without the gift
It can cause fear.

"I Don't Matter"
(Run Away Child, Run Away - Part One)

I was always looking for somewhere to hide, to be invisible. I can remember hiding in closets, under the bed, behind the couch, high up in trees, but never in the basement. The basement was damp and dark, full of shadows where danger could be lurking. There was a strong conflict between wanting to be noticed, yet fearing being noticed because it would bring about the wrong kind of attention. Hiding was safer, staying under the radar and just trying to do what was necessary to be accepted.

When I was four or five, I ran away. I don't remember the exact cause of my running away, just the feeling that I had to escape. I do wonder if it was the beginning of the time of sexual molestation; perhaps I was trying to get someone to pay attention and intervene. However, it could just have easily been my brother being mean to me or my sister resenting having to watch me, my frustration at feeling that my parents ignored me, or all of the above. All I remember is thinking, "I'll show them; I'll leave." I took my little dolly suitcase and ran across the church parking lot adjacent to our house to the woods on the other side. I was gone for some time, maybe hours. I walked along the stream, stopping when there were little waterfalls or pools of water where I could see bugs or fish. Nature has always been a place where I can find peace and get centered. At some point, I went home. No one had even noticed that I was gone. I am certain that this is the main event that caused me to believe I didn't matter. From then on, whenever I was ignored or not heard, it was reinforced.

One of my favorite things to do as a child, and even a young adult, was find a tall tree and climb as high as possible. I would sit there, unseen by others, watching whatever was happening in our yard or the neighbors' yards. Many times no one knew I was there. There was a stillness and peace that I craved. I would also ride my bike for hours, going as far as possible, where no one could bother me; I was free! When I was in the heights of the trees, or riding to faraway places, I was connected to nature. The painful reality of my familial existence was no longer in my consciousness.

There were many, many instances where the core belief and harassing voice saying "I don't matter" would manifest later in my life, where I would subonsciously create situations to "prove" that I didn't matter to others, acting out in ways where I knew they would not, could not, love me, to give proof to this core belief.

The enemy seeks to kill, steal and destroy (John 10:10) the very life and destiny God intended for us. He begins at a very young age.

Today I hear a different voice. The voice of the Lord comes to me and says, I knew you before time began, you were with me in Christ Jesus before I sent you to the earth for my Glory to be seen through your life.

> *"For we are his workmanship, created in Christ Jesus unto good works, which God hath before ordained that we should walk in them." Ephesians 2:10 (KJV)*

I matter.

"There is Something Wrong with You"

Soon after I was born, my mother noticed that there was something wrong with my left leg. I was told later that she thought a nurse dropped me. (I always thought my mother might have actually done it but said a nurse did it because she never looked me in the eyes when telling the story.) A few years ago, I had many tests done and the doctor told me that it was a congenital defect — I am actually missing a nerve that is normally connected between the left foot and leg.

As I grew, there was a noticeable limp of my left leg and my parents took me to the doctor when I was around four or five (it seems there were lots of things that happened to me at this age, forging my identity). I was forced to strip to my underwear and walk back and forth in the room with the doctor and my parents, with them staring at me, then talking about the problem — what was "wrong with me." I became very self-conscious about my body at that time, feeling ashamed at something being wrong with me.

Another significant, damaging event occurred when I was around ten years of age. I was very self-conscious and withdrawn at that age. The Bishop was visiting the church and one of the members was having a reception for him at their home. While there, he kept staring at me, then he turned to my parents and said, "You are going to have problems with that one." His voice of authority confirmed what I already believed — there was something wrong with me!

Yet the voice of the Lord says, You are loved, you are mine, I created you for my Glory. I loved you before you were born, I created you in My image; you are fearfully and wonderfully made!

"I will praise thee; for I am fearfully and wonderfully made marvelous are thy works; and that my soul knoweth right well." Psalms 139:14 (KJV)

You Are My Dove

Formed for glory, perfect and whole
Your spirit I formed, before your soul.
Let nothing hinder your view of My love
Beautiful and precious, you are my dove.

False Identity
(Or Perversion of Purpose)

When I was between the ages of four and six, I was sexually molested. It changed my view of self and relationships significantly. There was an older teenage boy, a neighbor who was very close to the family and who came from a family that was well known and respected in the church. My older siblings spent a lot of time with him. In fact, sometimes when my siblings were busy with other things he was given the authority to oversee us. He began to take me aside, in the basement and attic, and teach me about the differences between boys and girls: verbally, pictorially and then physically. I liked getting attention. However, this repeated exposure and conditioning took place when I was very young. It brought sexuality into my identity.

My mother found us one day when I was six and took me aside, telling me that those types of things are only supposed to happen when a man and woman get married. I felt ashamed, and at the same time angry because this person had actually taken interest in me and spent time with me. At that young age it seemed to me that the only person who paid attention to me was being taken away. I interpreted this as a great rejection from my mother and solidified my belief that she didn't really love me or understand me. The experience was never talked about in my family and I have no idea if my mother even told my father. The teenage boy was still involved with our family, although he never molested me again. The relationship became one of neighbors only towards me.

It is interesting to me that the enemy tempted Eve to doubt God by saying that He was withholding good from her. I felt that my mom was withholding good from me, although this was clearly something that was not good for me and she was right for stopping it. Nevertheless, the seeds of distrust of my mom were firmly planted. I already didn't trust my dad because he was very erratic in his moods and I never knew from one minute to the next if he would be kind or mean. He had his own struggles, as did my mom. When he was kind he was wonderful and funny, but he could be very acerbic and belittling, quite cruel in his words.

My family was very traditional in the sense that the woman did all the household duties even if she worked outside the home (which my mom did). I observed that my mother often would do and say things to pacify my father's moods, even if it meant lying to him and then doing something else. That was also confusing to me. When I was coming of age, my mother told me that wives needed to make sure their husband's sexual needs were met or they would find another way. There was an unspoken implication that they could not be controlled and that the woman's role was to make sure her husband's needs were met. Coupled with the molestation by an older boy who sometimes was "in charge" of me, I learned that women were to meet the needs of men.

When I was pubescent, we were all seated at the kitchen table eating dinner. I got up to get something, and my dad commented on my hips swaying as I went across the room, "Look at those hips move; you will make some man very happy one day." This, of course, reinforced the belief that I was made for others' (men's) enjoyment. This, combined with my reality that it was the one way I got attention and affection, would manifest in disastrous ways in the years to come. The perversity in our home and molestation I experienced at such a young age, combined with the strong religious mores instilled in us, created a warped view in my mind of God's design and intentions.

The emptiness I felt, and the shame that I was "bad" needed to be filled. I turned to food; that was an accepted pacifying tool in our home. We were offered cookies when crying to make it all better. I became compulsive in behavior, whether eating or repetitive actions, such as counting my steps. It was a way to try and maintain control in a dysfunctional, out of control home.

The sexualization of children brings great pain to my heart. Childhood should be a time of innocence, playing and enjoying life. Homes should be safe places for children where children feel loved and nurtured, where they see the unconditional love of God modeled and are free to try new things as they grow and develop. Ideally, they should be taught and shown that they are precious and unique, a gift from God with a great purpose for their life. Human trafficking has become one of the biggest businesses of the cartels and gangs, and children are a hot commodity. The perverting of God's purpose for life pains me, and I know it pains the heart of God Himself.

"But whose shall offend one of these little ones which believe in me, it were better for him that a millstone were hanged about his neck, and that he were drowned in the depth of the sea." Matthew 18:6 (KJV)

I hear the voice of the Lord say, **"You are precious in my sight; you bring me joy, you are my delight."**

Come to Me

My child, I am calling
Come to me
Let me fill you with love
And set you free

Free from the lies
That cloud your eyes
From seeing me,
To realize

That you are precious
In my sight
I created you;
You are my delight.

Conditional Love

I was a great student. I spent my elementary and junior high years alternating between trying to be perfect, so my parents would love me, and trying not to be perfect, so I would be "normal" and accepted by my peers. My obsessive-compulsive nature worked to my advantage in school. I always got straight A's but it never seemed to be enough. I didn't receive the affirmation I needed.

Up until 6th grade, I didn't mind being "different" but with the onset of puberty, that changed. Boys and girls started becoming meaner, and cliquish. I earned the nickname "Brainy Laney" and I was mortified. I hated anything drawing attention to myself; it was bad enough being a preacher's kid.

Worse, I won the "Best Student of the Year" award in 6th grade! I had to walk all the way from the back of the room to the stage with people whispering in shock. I was so shy and trying to stay under the radar, keeping my smarts hidden, that people (myself included) thought the very vocal and smartest boy in the class was going to get the award. In fact, he had started to stand up before they called my name!

My parents never had friends that I could see, so we kids didn't really learn how to socialize. We had groups of people from the church over occasionally, but my parents were in their "church" mode and putting on the right face. In fact, what I learned from my parents about right and wrong was that there were certain behaviors that were unacceptable for Christians, and especially for preacher's families. We weren't told at home why things were wrong or right, but that we had to act right because we were the preacher's family. Rebellion was beginning to stir inside. The voice of doubting my parents' wisdom (really God's wisdom) began to speak: "They are just trying to keep you from having fun." "Why do you have to have different rules than other kids." "You didn't ask to be a preacher's kid."

I still tried to be perfect for my parents, to win their acceptance and love, for a few more years.

Of course, now I know that none are perfect, that all sin and fall short of the Glory of God (Romans 3:23). That is why Jesus died for our sins, because of the Father's great love for us and desire that we be reconciled to Him. I know that parents are to love their children, not provoke them, but to bring them up in the nurture and admonition of the Lord (Ephesians 6:4). Oh, the fallen world that we are in. Now that I have raised children, and see my children raising my grandchildren, I understand so much more.

Perfect

I hear the voice of the Holy One
"The only one perfect is my Son.
My love for you cannot be earned,
Neither will you ever be spurned.
You are perfectly made, formed by Me.
Look to My Son and be set free.
Come close to Me and you will see
My love that continues eternally

His Presence Speaks with a Silent Voice

Although I did not receive Jesus into my heart as Lord and Savior until many years later, there were certain things that I was taught as a child, in church and through my parents. These were seeds of Truth buried in darkness until God's perfect timing.

One truth held deep within is the belief that God is omnipresent — He is everywhere all the time. I was taught that He was always watching and knew everything I did. To a child, I suppose this was sort of like the song about Santa Claus "...he sees you when you're sleeping...he knows when you're awake...so you better be good, for goodness' sake," but I was always aware of the existence of an Eternal God. I remember pondering how it could be that someone could be everywhere all the time; the mystery of God's all-encompassing being.

I was very conscious of the awesomeness, the majesty of creation. I believe creation spoke to me of God's existence, as I always had peace and "other-worldliness" cognizance when I was in nature settings. In my mid-childhood years, I went bicycling often and also went for long walks alone down the railroad tracks into the forested areas where there was a flowing stream.

Although forbidden to go down there (we had a minimum security prison nearby, as well as a mental hospital where there were frequent "escapes"), I was drawn and could not stay away. I loved being in the midst of towering trees, dappled light creating patterns on the diverse shades and textures surrounding me; with birds of all types singing their songs, chipmunks and squirrels scampering and chattering. I was unafraid until I found an encampment and signs of a recent campfire. After that, I never returned. "Something" told me it was no longer a safe place.

Even in my teenage years, when I was blatantly rebellious and disdained anything pertaining to "religion," I often was overwhelmed by majestic beauty when our family vacationed. The Grand Canyon, Yellowstone, Yosemite, the Tetons, Big Sur, the ocean...these stirred something deep within that I could not explain.

There was a moment when I was around 10 years old that the presence of the Lord came near to me, although I didn't know what or who it was at the time. As part of my upbringing, I memorized the Lord's Prayer. I can remember saying the Lord's Prayer nightly. One night I was reciting it, and I became very aware of an overwhelming Presence in the room, full of warmth and peace. I remember it as if it were yesterday. I lay there pondering and amazed, wondering what it could be. I am certain it was the Holy Spirit bearing witness to the Lord Jesus Christ, although I didn't know it then. Some don't believe that Holy Spirit moves in our lives until we are saved, but Jesus stated that *"No man can come to me, except the Father which hath sent me draw him; ad I will raise him up at the last day."* John 6:44 (KJV) I know that in looking back over my life, I can see His continual drawing me unto Himself.

"The LORD hath appeared of old unto me, saying, Yea, I have loved thee with an everlasting love; therefore with lovingkindness have I drawn thee." Jeremiah 31:3 (KJV)

Creator

Your voice cries out,
Though silently;
The beauty of nature says,
"Look and see."

Intricate and awesome
You made all things
The night sky with magnificence sings
A holy reverence it brings.

Heaven and all of creation
declare your being
Creator of all, all knowing' all seeing
Hallowed be thy name.

The Alluring Voice of the Counterfeit
(Run Away Child, Run Away - Part Two)

When I was fourteen, we vacationed in Virginia Beach, Virginia. Hormones were kicking in; my body was changing, and I was starting to notice boys and to want to be noticed by them! My family wasn't beach oriented; in fact, I never saw Maryland's beach until I was married to my first husband! I had seen some of California's beaches when we visited relatives, and been to lake shores, and occasionally the Chesapeake Bay beaches, but this was our first vacation at a "real" beach, spending a whole week.

This was also the summer prior to Woodstock. The hippie movement had begun and I didn't have a clue. Music had been changing over the last few years. I had seen some performed on The Ed Sullivan Show, and I had started listening to Rock and Roll — the Beatles, Rolling Stones, the Animals, etc., and was drawn to the sounds and the words. My older sister loved Elvis Presley and she had been dating boys that had that same vibe.

One of the things we did that summer was visit a nearby mall, and there was a "Head Shop" (store of psychedelic stuff) that we investigated. Oh my gosh, I was hooked by the music, the colors, the *feeling*, the camaraderie of the people that were in there, a secretive, forbidden lure of something outside of the norm that was very appealing to something inside me that I hadn't known existed. Some seeds were beginning to take root.

That year in school (eighth grade) we had been given an assignment in Comparative Religion class to research and report on a religion different from our own. I chose to study Tao. It appealed to me as very simplistic and nature oriented — everything part of each other and respecting (revering) all, and allowing "it" to work life out naturally. During my research, I came across something about Timothy Leary (a Psychologist and Harvard researcher and lecturer who advocated the use of LSD in therapy).

I remember reading that some people said they were able to see, hear, and experience God under LSD. Wow! I wanted that! More seeds, planted at a time when I was seeking the meaning of life. It seemed pointless to me, everyone doing things for what purpose? What was the meaning? Why was I born? What was I here for?

This was a very challenging time for me; it was a tumultuous year. My best friend and I had grown apart, not having any classes together, and I didn't really have any friends, just classmates. There was a boy who I liked and he liked me, but one day he said, "I could be your boyfriend if you'd lose weight." Ouch. I was probably 20 pounds overweight at the time. This spoke volumes to me about what it takes to have a boyfriend. Another significant event in the same category was that same year, during a lunch period. I was sitting at a table with some other girls, and there was a cute boy at the next table. He was staring at me. I heard him ask a girl sitting at his table, "Who is that girl? She's really cute." She responded, "Oh, you don't want anything to do with her; she's a preacher's kid!"

Immediately, my mind reeled with the injustice of my lot in life. I would never have a boyfriend, and I didn't ask to be a preacher's kid! It was a turning point to me. I wanted to change my identity and didn't know how. I was fed up with my home life being so meaningless – my older brother and sister were gone (Joy working, David in ROTC in Georgia, then at University of Pennsylvania for his Masters). I seemed to just be a bother to my parents; they were constantly annoyed with me and my increasingly sulky attitude (I felt fat, ugly, misunderstood, ignored and alone). My younger sisters were best friends with each other and I rarely did anything with them except have to watch them.

The earlier seeds of "I don't matter" were bearing fruit! I determined I would run away to Virginia Beach and get a new identity, try out new things, maybe I'd find the meaning and purpose to life and perhaps something that gave me value. It is amazing to me, in looking back, that I was so lacking a bond with my family that I thought they would not even care that I was gone. My best friend was supposed to go with me; we'd been planning it together, but the morning of (the day after my 15th birthday) she told me that she couldn't because it would hurt her mom too much. I didn't understand that. I could not relate. I was convinced my parents did not love me, want me, or need me, nor did anyone else in my family. I felt my brother loved me, even in the twisted teasing, and sometimes mean way that he had in actions; I knew he loved me, but he was gone away into his own life.

So, I took my savings (accumulation of weekly allowance) and another $20 from my dad's dresser, and some clothes in a bag, walked to the town where the Greyhound bus had a scheduled stop and got on the bus. I was afraid I'd be seen walking there along the main road or when I got to the bus stop, by someone who knew me (we lived in a rural, small town). I left some kind of a note, probably something like, "I'll be fine. Don't come looking for me. I need to do this." Or it could as easily have said, "I love you but have to do this to find myself." I don't remember.

The bus landed in a seedy part of Virginia Beach, crowded, smoky, noisy and confusing. Immediately a kind-looking young man approached me. I will call him Mike; truly, I don't remember his name. He seemed to be in his early twenties. He introduced himself and somehow convinced me that he was okay. I remember him telling me I was in a dangerous area and offering to take me to a safe place near his house (he lived with his parents) where I could spend the night. He said he would help me find somewhere to stay the next day. He seemed safe, so on I went. Near his house, in a normal-looking middle-class neighborhood, was a slightly wooded area where I spent the night on the ground. I can tell you I didn't really sleep. I was very alert and aware, a little scared. I kept singing Beatles songs in my head, like "Yesterday" and "Lady Madonna" until the sun came up. I think he may have brought me some food and something to drink; I can't really remember.

The next morning, he came and off we went on his motorcycle to the "real" Virginia Beach, i.e. the beach area. We rode around looking for a rental. In front of an older beach cottage was a handmade sign, "Room for Rent." He pulled his bike up to the curb and we got off. He said he would do the talking and take care of it. I didn't have much thought about it; I was going along with all my experiences, just letting life happen. The owner was a grandmotherly-looking woman. They discussed the rent, which was week-to-week. She showed me the room, which had a bed, dresser and nightstand. The woman didn't have many questions, didn't ask how old I was or why I was alone at such an obviously young age. I don't even remember; "Mike" may have told her I was a relative visiting for the month. She laid down the rules (what time I had to be "home" by, room and bath only, no kitchen privileges, although I could use the front room for visitors, but not too many and no loud parties). He gave her some money and that was that.

I was in Virginia Beach for six weeks. This was a very strange time, in part because during that six-week period I can only remember eating half a submarine sandwich, having an ice cream cone and drinking some sodas.

So, in essence, I was on a six week fast. I lost 30 pounds, my virginity, and became an inductee into the hippie movement through pot and LSD. I spent my days wandering the streets of Virginia Beach, trying to engage passersby by flipping a peace sign, smiling or saying "hi" to them. I wanted to see what kind of reaction I would get from the different things.

One day there was a white van that pulled up alongside me and a man opened the door and grabbed me, pulling me in. I remember the song "White Room" was playing on the radio. There were a lot of people in the van, smoking pot, and some little kids playing on the floor. They told me they had a farm where a lot of people lived together and asked me if I wanted to go live with them, and I said, "No, that's cool, but I have a place." So they opened the door at the next intersection and out I went.

A few days later a much scarier experience happened. A fancy convertible stopped as I was walking and an older man grabbed me and pulled me into the back seat. There was another, older man driving. Both were probably in their late thirties (remember, I was barely 15 so they were old to me), and the sense I had was one of danger, unlike the time with the van. They began telling me that they had a really nice house on the beach, that I would have everything I needed or wanted, and all the drugs I could want. I sat paralyzed in fear, not saying anything. After five or ten minutes of their telling me what a wonderful life I would have with them, and my non-responsiveness, they asked me "How old are you, anyway?" "Something" told me I should lie, so I said, "14." They looked at each other and the driver said, "You know, I think we will take you back where we found you."

Mike came by every day after work and we smoked pot and went for rides to different places. The fact that he rode a motorcycle seemed to give him an immediate kinship with fellow motorcyclists — they were always stopping and talking with each other and became "brothers" by reason of bikes. We met up with three brothers who lived together in a beach cottage. They invited us to a party. The house was one block from the beach, and also on one of the main thoroughfares. There was a lot of alcohol, drugs and music. I did LSD for the first time. We all walked over to the ocean after a time, and I walked into the water, fully clothed in my jeans and t-shirt. It was no wonder that people were looking at me askance. I can still remember the troubled glances of some of the moms. I was invited to "stay" in this house rent-free, so I did. I was beginning to feel a little uncomfortable with the possessiveness of Mike towards me, although I didn't particularly want to be with someone else. I was starting to feel uncomfortable having sex with him because I didn't really have any feelings for him; he was a nice guy, but that was all. I didn't like the feeling of obligation or having expectations placed on me.

One afternoon I was outside and a police car driving by stopped in front of the house. The "guys" were on high alert (no pun intended) because they were selling pot. The officer got out and came over, showing us a picture of a runaway and asking if we had seen her. It was very odd and troubling, in that I was not ready to go home yet, and also that I was a runaway, but they didn't seem to be aware of that. In retrospect, it was even more troubling in that there was a five-state alert out on me and they didn't ask me any questions.

One day near the end of my time in Virginia Beach, the brothers and two others were bagging up pot for sale. I was in the room with them and one of the older men who was married began fondling me. I was very uncomfortable with this and he asked me what was wrong. I said, "You are married!" He said, "Well there's nothing wrong with eating steak for dinner but wanting a hamburger once in a while." I was very offended and disgusted at his immoral thinking and left the room. That same night another man who came by later for partying, tried to "talk me into" having sex with him and he was a little pushier. It was starting to become scarier now, living this life.

As we neared the arrival of summer, the rent on the house was to be tripled, so it was time for them to move out. They offered to let me come along, and Mike offered to help me find another place, but I felt it was time to go home. Mike took me to an organization that helped runaways. The staff there told me that they would have to call my parents, and then when my parents came there would be a counseling session with a mediator. I was willing, so they made the call to my parents. My brother answered and when he heard my voice, he said, "Laney, is that really you? I thought you were dead." I was shocked. It honestly hadn't occurred to me that my family might actually think something terrible happened to me. I was so naive and self-absorbed.

My parents drove down the next day and we had the meeting. I remember they were shocked at my appearance. I had lost 30 pounds, I was braless and my clothes were hanging off me (my jeans were held up with a rope). In the meeting, I told them that I'd done drugs and had sex but not much else. On the ride home, they asked me more questions. They told me that they had been heartbroken, shocked, and very afraid. My dad had driven all the way to New York, combing the streets of Greenwich Village looking for me. There was a five-state alert and private detectives were searching for me. I found out that my younger sisters had been heartbroken, and cried day and night for me. My oldest sister recently told me that she felt very guilty when I left, that she hadn't taken an active interest in my life.

I thank God for His hand of protection. I felt "lucky" at the time, but now I know it was people praying for my safe return and God's divine plan and protection on my life. When I became a parent, especially when my kids were teenagers, I realized just how scary it was for my parents and siblings. It is hard to believe that my mental and emotional state were such that I honestly didn't think it would matter to anyone if I disappeared from their lives.

That summer my family traveled west. My dad would save some of his vacation time each year and every five years or so we would travel across the country to visit my Mom's side of the family. My mom was a teacher, so she always had the summer off. Her relatives were spread out from the East Coast to the South, to the Midwest and West Coast. These family trips were quite an experience for us all. My dad was extremely meticulous in his budgeting of time and money, and we were on a strict schedule and budget. Each day he would write down every expense and log every mile. If we went over in either area, we'd have to make it up the next day.

This summer only four of the kids were to accompany my parents...Joy was an adult now and working. David was still in college, but working part of the summer. He flew out to join us when we got to California. These trips were made before cars had air conditioning, and way before the internet. We would travel for a few days, stopping for the night and staying in whatever cheap motel was available, (us kids hoping for a pool) until we reached one of our destinations – a relative that I rarely saw so barely knew. If we were lucky, they had kids and we played with them. Otherwise, we sat around bored out of our minds and trying to behave while the adults visited.

Traveling in the car with four kids is never pleasant, but eight hours a day, days on end, is a nightmare! It was hot and the quarters were close. This trip wasn't as bad as a previous one where all five kids went and the youngest was a baby, but it was still challenging.

I was practicing my new identity this summer, dressing like a hippie and trying to maintain my newly acquired small size. When we got to California, I knew this is where I wanted to live one day. All the free spirits, especially in Big Sur, drew me like a moth to the light on the darkest night. We came in through the Tetons and travelled south to San Diego County, where my aunt and uncle and their children lived. The ocean, from the raw beauty of the coastline in Big Sur to the peaceful shorelines in San Diego County, I was hooked! This was my first clear impression of ocean life since the year before in Virginia Beach. My parents were not ocean people, but I clearly was. My soul craved the vastness, the rhythm of the waves and the mesmerizing, surging power. If I could have put words into what drew me to California, it would be "being one with nature and flowing with the vibe of life." I was rejecting the "busyness" of life full of rules and regulations that seemed meaningless, and California was calling my name. I longed to be free of what seemed to be bondage and routine with no purpose.

Whom the Son sets free is free indeed. Jesus tells us to become as little children, and there is true freedom when we understand what that means and can live as such. The enemy brings the counterfeit freedom disguised as a life of no rules, living for each moment. The reality is that little children are only truly free to explore when there are safe parameters in their life. A child with no boundaries will bring harm to himself. True freedom is living within the boundaries set by a loving father, knowing you will be taken care of and corrected when getting off course. A good father knows what the child needs.

*"He that hath no rule over his own spirit is like a city that
is broken down, and without walls." Proverbs 25:28 (KJV)*

Counterfeit

*The enemy lures us with his lies
Deceiving us as he tries
To shape our identity through pride and lust
Sowing seeds of doubt and distrust
Focusing on what we lack
We eat the fruit and get off track
There is an identity we are searching for
But there is only one way, one entrance, one door
To which our true self can be realized
And it isn't through the devil's lies
The Kingdom of God is full of light,
Creative beauty, spiritual sight
He is the Eternal One
Creator of the stars, moon and the sun
He draws us to Himself with hope
When we have reached the end of our rope
We know there is something more
He calls us to what He created us for
A new identity is in store*

Trip, Trip, Tripping Away
(Run Away Child, Run Away ~ Part Three)

The first day of school in 9th grade, with my new identity of hippie, I met my first husband. I saw him at the bus stop and I was immediately drawn to him. He was very handsome, and there was a something about him that drew me like a magnet – our eyes connected and "that's all she wrote," as they say. We were inseparable from that moment on. He lived within walking distance from my house, a few streets behind my best friend's house. It was perfect. We rode the bus together to and from school, and I was allowed to "see" him three times a week; the other days I "went for a walk." His mom and stepfather worked, and his sister was home after school also, but I guess they had an agreement of sorts. We just spent almost all the time in his room listening to music, making out and getting stoned.

I maintained my grades so that I could see my boyfriend; I could not get enough of him and thoughts of him consumed every moment. Being in love had to be the purpose of life, and I was wanted, desired, beautiful! This was the drug that filled every need; the other drugs were just an accompanying factor. I just wanted to merge myself with him and stay cocooned in his room forever.

Eventually we did acid; mostly we were smoking pot and hash, and doing speed sometimes. I loved LSD. It was as if another reality opened up and it was so much better than real life – the colors had voices and the music had color; everything vibrated with a life force multiplied the more you stared at it. Of course, that backfired when it was ugly or scary; then it became a "bad trip."

There were, naturally, many negative effects to LSD as well. I became very withdrawn, as I preferred to live in this other state. I lost what little connection I had with my family members. I eventually got to the point that I was so introspective that I seemed to be perpetually "stoned" as I could sit and stare for what seemed like hours, listening to voices and music in my head. Drugs have a voice, many voices. At one point I remember not even being able to complete a sentence, in part because my mind was somewhere else, listening to the other voices! We did LSD hundreds of times, at least every weekend, within the course of two years. Someone had started renting out a hall where live music was played every Friday night...this became the place to be. Parents would drop off their` kids, and we'd all be tripping listening to music. Eventually, this became problematic when people started bringing in alcohol and PCP.

This all came to a crashing halt the fall of 11th grade. We decided to do acid the first day of school. Once we got to school, we could barely make it up the bleachers in the auditorium where we were all gathered – the steps were in 3-D and we didn't have 3-D glasses! We almost tripped coming down them (pun intended). We couldn't read our class schedules; the depth of the letters made them all blurry. So we decided to ditch the rest of school. We left and were walking down the road and didn't know what to do. How could we go back to school the next day? Our parents would find out and we'd be grounded (at the least). We decided to run away together, walked home and gathered some things (a few clothes, some money and drugs) and took a Greyhound bus to Florida.

We arrived at the Greyhound depot in Miami a few days later. Miami did not match the picture we had in our minds. I didn't realize that Miami Beach and Miami were different. Not that it would have mattered, because that's where the bus went. By the time we got there, it was late in the afternoon and we needed to find a motel. We were in a very bad section of town. A man walked by bleeding from his chest as he had just been shot, telling my boyfriend to get me out of there, that it was not a good place for young women. We entered a seedy motel and got a room. I had never seen water bugs and cockroaches so big in my life, or so many! I don't think we slept much. It was a little scary. So, the next day we hitchhiked into Miami Beach and were halfway across the bridge when the police drove up. Miami Beach doesn't like hippies.

The police played "good cop, bad cop" and I spilled the beans when one of them told me my boyfriend had admitted to them we had drugs. He hadn't, of course, but I was very naïve and believed them. My boyfriend was charged as an adult; he was 17 (by one month) and I was 16. I was hysterical as they took him away to jail and took me to a facility for juvenile delinquents.

The next few days were a nightmare for me. The facility setup was like a jail, with a room having a barred door that was locked at night. There was a bunkbed and dresser in the room, although we weren't allowed to wear our own clothes. When I arrived I was strip-searched and given their clothes to wear. Many of the girls in this facility were very troubled. One had pushed her baby brother down the stairs and killed him. My "roommate" used the bottom dresser drawer as a toilet in the middle of the night when no one responded to her request to use the bathroom. I cried day and night. At the end of the week, my boyfriend's father came to visit me and get us out. I was so distraught I did not recognize him; I thought he was the lawyer.

When we came home, there were discussions that I don't really remember, and we were able to continue seeing each other and return to school. We really "cooled down" on the drugs. We stopped taking LSD and speed, and returned to only smoking pot and hash.

This section was titled "Trip, Trip, Tripping Away" as a play on words. Obviously, tripping refers to LSD. Equally true, though, is that it caused tripping in another sense — falling down. The enemy always has a counterfeit of what God has in the heavenly realms, in the Spirit for us. There was a longing in me for the supernatural, for the depths, heights, and widths of experience that cannot be found in the natural realm. All of the things that seemed enhanced by drugs are those very things that occur when in the Shekinah Glory of God!!! The colors are brighter, sounds vibrate to a level of light, light can have sounds; we see and hear things in our inner man of the Spirit that come to us straight from the throne of God. Not only that, but when you are walking in the purposes of God for your life, there is a satisfaction that fills in a way that no drug can match.

"Let me take you higher" was the song of the time, yet how much higher does God take us into the realms of Glory!

Higher Heights

If only you could see and know
The heights to which your spirit can go
In Him who inhabits eternity.
For only in Him can you truly see
All that in your heart you long to be
Is found in the riches of His Glory.
All else pales and fades away
As certainly as night follows the day.

Devastating Loss

In early 1972, I became pregnant. This was a shocking time for me. Getting pregnant wasn't shocking; obviously that can happen when you are having unprotected sex. The reactions of our parents was the shocking part. We wanted to get married and I assumed everyone would understand because we were in love! Abortion was never even considered as a possibility by me; although I didn't really buy into Christianity, I did believe that there was a God and that life begins at conception. I was always very cognizant of the incredible magnificence of creation in all of its forms, and the reality that it had to be by design.

We decided to tell my parents together. We approached my Dad and I told him I was pregnant, and my boyfriend said we wanted to get married. My dad said he would give it thought. We told my mom and she turned white as a ghost, and seemed very upset. She said we would talk later. Separately, alone, in the car, I remember vividly her response. She was furious, then said, "Well, we'll just have to get an abortion then." I was shocked. I could not believe what came out of her mouth! I was shocked that she would even consider abortion as an option (being a religious woman), and appalled that she would take it upon herself to make a decision like that about my life, especially since my boyfriend and I were in love.

My boyfriend told his parents separately, and alone. They both wanted me to have an abortion, which was also shocking to me, as his father was Catholic and his mother Jewish. All the parents decided to meet with my boyfriend to discuss. I was told that I could not attend because I was too emotional. Now that I wasn't doing drugs (and also being pregnant), my emotions were running full force. I was very passionate in my stances, and I was furious and incredulous that something so important, that should have been my decision, was being taken out of my hands completely. If I had been thinking rationally, I would have realized that no one could have forced me to have an abortion...they would not have drugged me, taken me to an abortionist and tied me to a table. The result of the "discussion" was that we would get married. My Dad said we could live in our house, in the attic (my older brother and sister had both used it but were now out of the house), so we could continue to go to school.

We married in May of that year. The following month, when I was barely five months pregnant, my water broke. We went to the hospital and found out after examination that the umbilical cord was wrapped around the baby's neck and he was dead. They had to induce labor, and I had to deliver a dead baby. To say that this was devastating is a gross understatement. It felt like I cried for months. Inwardly, I'm not sure I ever stopped. It was a number of years before I was willing to try to get pregnant again; I was so afraid of losing another.

Many people said things to try and comfort me, such as "Well, it's for the best." That isn't very comforting to a person grieving the loss of a baby that they will never see, this side of heaven. It was doubly hard because one of my husband's cousins was pregnant at the same time as me, so I had to act happy for them when the baby was born.

There was part of me that died at that time; it was the death of innocent love, the death of a core connection of intimacy. A part of me was buried in the aftermath of grief. I did not know the Lord at this time, and I could not receive comfort from anyone around me.

> "*Thus saith the LORD; A voice was heard in Ramah, lamentation, and bitter weeping; Rachel weeping for her children refused to be comforted for her children, because they were not.*" Jeremiah 31:15 (KJV)

Beckoning

How I longed to pour upon you
My everlasting love
To cover you with peace
And lavish comfort from above.
I was speaking to you,
Although you could not hear;
Ever drawing closer,
Beckoning you near.

Interlude
(A Tale of Two Cities)

After graduation, we entered the "real" world and the responsibilities of life as an adult. It is here that my issues began to surface, interacting with others outside of the protected environment of home and school.

My siblings and I received an inheritance from a distant relative. My husband and I used mine to buy a used car and for his enrollment in a year-long drafting school in Pennsylvania. We moved to Pennsylvania and lived in a row home in downtown Allentown. It was an interesting location. We lived within walking distance of both a bar and a church, neither of which we entered. The noise from the bar sometimes kept us up until they closed at 2:00 in the morning, with the church bells waking us the next morning. I got a job at the County of Lehigh, doing clerical work.

During this brief time (nine months) a lot happened. We weren't doing drugs during this time, and it was a time of us becoming very close in many ways. At the same time, many of my issues rose to the surface. My husband's lung collapsed for the first time here. He was having a lot of pain and difficulty breathing one day. It became worse and he asked to go to the hospital. I was so scared. They put him in intensive care after operating. When I saw him with all the tubes coming out of his chest and in his arms, I almost fainted. The attending nurse made me sit down and gave me smelling salts. I could not handle the sight of him with tubes and blood, and the fear of losing him was overwhelming.

During my husband's recovery period, I developed what the doctor diagnosed as "vertigo." I could not work; I was dizzy all the time. Neither of us could drive; I could not drive because of the dizziness and my husband couldn't drive because he couldn't use one arm. So I would maneuver the steering wheel while he sat behind the wheel so that we could go to the store, do our laundry, go the doctor...the normal things of life.

We didn't have a lot of money during this time. Sometimes I would do our laundry in the bathtub and hang ropes from door to door so the wet clothes could be draped on the ropes to dry. We didn't have a yard at the row home.

Once a classmate came by to visit my husband. I was shy and fearful, full of insecurity and inferiority, and I hid in the bathroom the whole time he was there. I have no idea what I would have done if he had needed to go to the bathroom!

When we moved back to Maryland, we lived in an apartment for a while, then the house my husband had grown up in. His father was living in a different home with his second wife and this house was vacant. We were doing drugs again during this time, and most of my memories of this time are a blur. We eventually bought a row home in Baltimore, where both of us were working. I was working for the State of Maryland at the Bureau of Vital Records, and eventually was offered a supervisory position which I turned down because I was not interested in having that level of responsibility.

I named this section a tale of two cities because we were in two physically different locations during this timeframe, but also because it truly was a very disparate time of drug-free versus drug-numbed. I remember clearly the times we had without drugs, and how happy I was then, versus the times when we were using drugs again. Although I enjoyed the fantasy world, the escape from my issues, deep down I was disconnected and despondent.

Hiding

Your heart cries out but you hide the pain
And try to create a new refrain
To the song of sadness within your soul,
Searching for something to make you whole.
My love alone can fill that place
And heal the wounds, leaving not a trace.
Look to me, seek My face
I long to fill you with My embrace.

Motherhood
(Inferiority Rears its Ugly Head)

When I was 22 years old, our first baby, Cara, was born. I was still working at the State of Maryland as a clerical employee and we were living in downtown Baltimore. We had started smoking pot again, and a few other things here and there. My husband would often talk about a female co-worker... he said that she wasn't the smartest person in the world, but she was very happy. He concluded that smarter people were generally less happy than stupid ones. I was pretty smart, so I assumed he was making comparisons and I fell short. This was my filter of inferiority. ("There's something the matter with you.") I was uncertain about where we were going in our marriage, and wanted to quit drugs and change our life. I hoped that having a baby would change things.

As soon as I found out I was pregnant, I quit doing all drugs and drinking, and became obsessed with health. I was so afraid of losing this baby. When Cara was born, I was even more scared. I realized I didn't know anything about babies, and had no idea how to do this! I was too full of pride and fear to ask for help; I thought it was an inadequacy on my part; that somehow women should automatically know what to do. Once again, the "there's something wrong with you" voice came in. My mom seemed to be the perfect mother; she always seemed to know what to do. Other moms looked so self-assured and "natural" in their mothering.

However, there were moments where I would hold Cara in the middle of the night and she would stop nursing and just stare at me. I felt such love, and a very strong bond, as if we were one. It was overwhelming and a little scary when I thought about how this perfect little person was my responsibility and I had no idea what to do. I loved those moments of connection though, when in the still of the night it was just us. I wanted to bring her into bed, but I was so afraid that I'd roll over on her and crush her.

I tried to do everything perfectly. Everything became about Cara; my life revolved around taking care of her. Our families were thrilled; Cara was the first grandbaby on both sides of the family and we were in high demand. I started to feel like we had no time together as a family. My husband worked

Monday through Friday and every weekend someone wanted to come visit; I felt pressure to entertain. He loved having people over, while I always felt it was a strain because I didn't measure up to others and wasn't very good at small talk.

My husband was still smoking pot and now he was growing it in our basement. He was also talking about starting his own business and that scared me. I really valued security and didn't trust that we'd be able to make it financially. I started looking for a way out of the pressure of fear and inferiority, and the constant pressing demands of others on our time. Somehow I thought that moving (running away) would make things better, with less pressure to be perfect. I had no idea at the time it was something within me.

Fearful

You run, you hide behind a mask
Trusting no one, fearful to ask
For fear that you will be shamed again;
Those wounds are buried so deep within.
In the course of life you will see
My love can heal and set you free.

California Dreaming
(Run Away Child, Run Away ~ Part Four)

One day when perusing the classifieds, there was an ad for a drafting job in California. I told my husband about it and he agreed to apply for it. His field was in such high demand that they flew us out for the interview. We moved to San Diego when Cara was six months old. I just knew that this was where I would finally be at peace and be able to find fulfillment. California was hippie-heaven in my mind, and we'd have a new start. Instead, I became more isolated and felt very alone.

I had one relative nearby, an aunt — my mom's sister, but we only saw her about every six months or so. She has truly been a California grandmother to my children, but I was unable to express what was inside to receive true support from anyone. The first winter here it must have rained nearly every day. I thought it would never end. I was depressed all the time. I was unhappy again. Whenever I'd want to talk about problems, my husband would want to avoid them. His parents had always fought, so he did everything he could to avoid conflict. I always felt inadequate. I felt he didn't understand me, nor really want to. I started to doubt that he truly "loved" me.

My husband was very outgoing and social, and he loved parties, whereas I was an introvert with little to no social skills and large group gatherings (especially parties) were very hard for me. I hated small talk. It all seemed so meaningless. He made a friend at work who was married and had children, one only a few years older than Cara. The husband didn't do drugs, but his wife did. She was really into feminism and they both enjoyed going to Black's Beach (a nude beach). Pretty soon I was smoking pot again. Their marriage was struggling, and the wife began asking me probing questions about my marriage, and why I was living for my child and husband and not thinking of myself at all.

The friends convinced us to try out Black's Beach. The first time there I was mortified and kept my head down most of the time. They laughed and joked about it. Over time, I started to question my beliefs — well, what was wrong with the human body? Everybody else seemed to enjoy the freedom and lack of inhibitions. It went along with my "wanting to be free" thinking.

Coupled with my filter of "there's something wrong with you" and trying to fit in because of that filter, over a short period of time I gave myself over to it completely.

Our second child, Sara, was born when Cara was not quite two. I was so scared the whole time I was pregnant with Sara. It was challenging with a toddler and having no family support or friends; I really questioned if I would be able to manage it. When Sara was born, I fell in love with her immediately. She was such a delight! However, it was also a really difficult time. Having two children in diapers, different nap times, constant demands every moment of every day, no family or friends for support, and my inferiority and desire to be "perfect" in all areas, was a recipe for disaster.

I felt bad for Cara having to share me and that it wasn't fair for Sara because she would never have me to herself as Cara had. I had no time to myself (not that I would have known what to do with it). I resented that my husband could go to work and have that "escape" and that he seemed happy all the time. He had a natural, easy-going way of being that was foreign to me. I tried to "become" that, but it didn't work.

My mom came out after Sara was born, for a week. It was one of the first times I really felt she understood something about what I was going through. I could tell by her eyes that she knew first-hand how challenging it was and would be in the months ahead. Her first and second were only 14 months apart, so she had experienced that part of my difficulties.

We did start going to a church for a short time, as we wanted Sara baptized. My dad had baptized Cara before we moved to San Diego. The church had a weekly childcare "sharing" program where the moms could get some time alone. It was a two-hour program in the morning. There was a commitment of every mom once per month helping with childcare so the other moms could have the two-hour break. I didn't do that for long, maybe a few weeks, because I felt inadequate and "less than" all the other moms. I could not seem to relate to anyone and was fearful they would judge me if they really got to know me.

During this time we lived in a house that shared a yard with another property. There was a man in the other house that turned us on to meth.

Oh my; now I was *happy*. My mood was elevated and I liked it. I met a young woman with two small children that lived nearby and she was also doing it; I began doing meth with her a few times per week. This came to an abrupt end, as did our friendship, in a short period of time. They moved to East County. When I went to visit her, her husband was there and her face was bruised and swollen. She was very subdued in conversing with me, on guard and inhibited. I never saw her again. It was the first time I'd ever seen domestic violence up close and personal, and it wasn't pretty.

Also during this timeframe, I had an accident where my ring finger was cut and they had to remove my wedding ring. I felt at the time that it was fate showing me there was a break in our marriage. Sara was about six months old at the time, and I was bandaged and one-armed for a good six weeks. My mom came out for a week or so at the beginning to help.

Our friends divorced, but still spent a good deal of time together, trying to get along for their children's sake. They took the EST training (Erhard Seminars Training), which was touted as a transformative experience. It was all the rage in the 80's in Southern California. They eventually convinced us to do it. I went first. It was a two-weekend-long experience of being in a huge room with many other people and the speakers talking all day and night, speaking in a provocative, belittling way to cause your "issues" to arise and then look at them, with their "insight" added as to the reason for the issues. It began very early in the morning and went until nearly midnight (if I recollect correctly). There were very limited bathroom breaks and only one short meal break. I came out of that believing that everything we experience in our lives is determined by our beliefs; in other words, we create our own reality. I was angry. I felt that I'd been duped, brainwashed, misled by society. I wanted to live existentially if this was the case; no beliefs at all. Knowing what I know now, it was a combination of New Age/Eastern philosophies, Existentialism, brainwashing.

I began searching spiritually, reading books about Eastern religions and the occult. The "New Age" movement seemed to have answers to what I was searching for. Transcendental meditation, becoming one with the universe, and experiencing nirvana was the goal to life! I lived for my kids' naptimes; I would lay on the balcony and enter into a meditative state. Doors were opening and there was a higher level of consciousness to be attained through answer to my "life question" — what is the purpose of life?

Next thing I knew, my husband told me we were moving. He found a bigger house for us to rent, not too far away. It was a shock to me as I didn't even know he was looking! It was a beautiful modern house, and I was happy it was bigger, but it didn't have a yard and I resented not being involved in any of the decision making. He hadn't even asked my opinion or told me he was looking (although perhaps he had, but I was preoccupied with the children and didn't hear him). Once again, I felt I didn't matter.

His sister moved in with us, and now we had a built-in babysitter, so we started to go out dancing every weekend, drinking and doing more drugs. Dancing had been a big part of our connecting. I viewed dancing as the one way in which I could communicate what I was feeling. Dancing was a huge release of emotional conflict! It was definitely a form of sexual interplay between us, and when other men would want to dance with me it seemed my husband enjoyed others getting "turned on," but not going too far. Of course, we never talked about it so it could just as easily have been in my mind. I am well aware that I might have been projecting my feelings onto my husband. After all, I was the one with the sexualized identity. It would be many years before I could recognize and face that as a false identity with perversity at the root. I thought it was "who I was." Yet I had a strong moral code that conflicted with this...an internal time bomb waiting to explode.

One of my husband's friends started coming over when my husband wasn't home; he began flirting with me. My husband would invite him over with some others on Friday nights for poker and I prepared the snacks and sat around. The friend began engaging me emotionally, he was relating to me on a deep level that no one had ever done before. He didn't do drugs and was attractive, in a different "California surfer" kind of way. He wasn't really my "type" but I enjoyed the attention. When the others would "zone out" and my husband began nodding off, he would make innuendos and suggestive remarks and body language towards me.

Psychotic Break

My husband and I had a Saturday where the kids were being watched by either his sister or our friends (I don't remember). We took the day to go to the beach and took acid for the first time in years, then smoked pot.

Something snapped mentally after we smoked that pot. I began hearing voices; it was as if there were other voices in my head and they were in conflict. We were in the car getting ready to leave, and I was observing some surfers and thought about one, "He is cute." My husband seemed to address this thought, saying, "Oh, is that how it is going to be?" We didn't talk about it; I didn't ask him, "What do you mean?" I was scared and ashamed, guilty, and felt exposed because of thoughts that I was having. From that point on there was a separation between us, in the way I viewed us. The voices got worse. Others in our lives also now seemed able to "read my mind." I became very paranoid, thinking that everyone was playing mind games and they were trying to manipulate me. There were conflicting voices all the time. I felt like I was going crazy.

I also became convinced my husband was having an affair with a co-worker. We had gone to her house for a party and they disappeared into the back bedroom together. When I questioned him about it, he said they were doing cocaine, but I didn't believe him. I didn't feel loved or necessary; everything was being filtered through my internal beliefs of "I don't matter" and "There's something wrong with you." My inferiority and insecurity in myself and in our relationship convinced me that even if he wasn't having an affair now, it was only a matter of time. It wasn't the first time I wondered if he was having an affair, as I mentioned before about the "happy" co-worker. I had such inferiority and insecurity that I was jealous of everyone he was friendly with.

I was certain that even if he wasn't having an affair currently, he would leave me for someone else eventually because I wasn't a "happy" person. I didn't feel he understood me, subsequently reasoning he didn't really love me. I imagined him leaving me after having been married 25 years or so. A seed had been planted that he didn't really love me and would eventually leave me. Deep down, I knew that if he left me it would destroy me. I was jealous of every other woman who was in his life and saw them as being able to relate to him in ways I could not. I didn't know how to relate; I didn't really know who I was. I had spent all my life being as I saw others, and what I perceived was expected of me to get what I needed (my perception of love and acceptance), and I was face-to-face with the reality that it was empty and meaningless and I had no idea how to change that.

His flirtatious friend was over all the time, talking to me and getting to me by relating to me on a level that no one else had before. He seemed able to see into my soul about the things that were going on in my heart. The inevitable happened; I began to have feelings for him. He was meeting a need I didn't know I had! I was so confused. If I loved him, how could there be "one true love." I had based everything on the belief that my husband and I were the "match made in heaven," "soul mates," so how could this other man understand me better than my soul mate? I wanted my husband to see what was going on and fight for me. I was very conflicted, my soul in turmoil. I loved my children, I loved being a wife, but the culture and my "friends" were telling me that was wrong. They were saying that there was more to life than living for others, that I needed to begin living for myself, seeking my own pleasure and desires. My husband sensed my disconnection and dissatisfaction and suggested I babysit other kids so that we could have some extra money and I could still be home with the kids. I am sure he thought that I wasn't busy enough and needed more to do. It certainly kept me busy, but did nothing to occupy my mind or satisfy my searching soul.

I had quit all drugs and drinking after doing the EST training, and wanted my husband to. Honestly, I can't remember if he didn't want to or was unable to at the time. I was comparing him to his friend who seemed to have an inner strength that I admired. At the same time, during my times of meditation I was having visions. I "saw" myself in past lives, and the same dilemma was taking place in those — torn between two men and two realities. In each of them, I ran, as I could not decide and didn't want to hurt either one. I became convinced that this was my fate. I believe I was experiencing demonic influence; I was empty, open spiritually, a vessel ready for infiltration! Later, a psychologist told me that often when people are facing a crisis, their minds will fabricate things as a coping mechanism. That may be the medical community's opinion, and perhaps true in some cases, but I can tell you that what I was seeing seemed so real that I am convinced it was demons rather than my own mind. I know about fabrication, and this was more like being in a trance. I was angry and confused. I was racked with guilt for the feelings I was having for another man – his best friend, no less! I felt unfaithful even though I hadn't done anything with him. I became convinced that my "fate" was to be a free spirit, exercising free love and went to prove I was free by dancing at a nude club. At one point, I was in a car with a near stranger at the beach. I saw stars falling from the sky, the sea turned to blood, and there were hordes of people running through the streets screaming, "The end is near."

In hindsight, I can see that my behavior was motivated by a subconscious desire to force my husband to do something – fight for me or let me go, to make the decision for me and say he hated me; that would prove to me he didn't love me - just as I thought. Yet at the time, I was completely oblivious to any of this.

Now I can see clearly that there was a battle raging for my soul, though at the time I didn't know it. I heard two voices; one saying how much I loved the kids and they needed me and it would rip my heart out to leave; another saying I have to go, they'd be better off without me, they don't need me, I don't matter, anyone can do a better job raising them; that would show my husband what it would be like without me, etc.. I was torn between guilt and the love for my children. I had such conflicting feelings; I wasn't a heartless person and felt for my husband, yet the voices of condemnation and guilt, the voices that said I didn't matter and this was all part of my fate were constant. I felt I had to go, but was fearful to make a wrong decision.

One evening I told him he didn't really love me, but just needed me. He said, in anger, "I don't need you; I don't need anyone!" I was so hurt. How could he say that? I felt unappreciated, deeply wounded and confused. I wanted him to see what it was like to have to be with small children every day, not having adult conversations, living just to serve others. He made it seem so easy; he would come home from work and play with the kids and not understand why I was frustrated and impatient, why the house wasn't perfectly clean and organized.

I left, and took nothing with me but some clothes. Deep down, I didn't believe I deserved to have anything because I felt such guilt. I believe now that when we sin, our God-given conscience knows that we need to be punished.

In retrospect, I know that I wanted my husband to fight for me. Instead, his passivity reinforced my conviction that I wasn't loved or needed, that I didn't matter, and there was something wrong with me. One of my core internal beliefs was manifesting in my life: I didn't matter. I did not know at the time that I was yearning for the unconditional love that only God can give. I wanted someone to hear my heart cry. I know now that when a lie of the enemy is manifesting in your reality, this is where God wants to come in and heal you of that wound. I only knew the pain at the time, and I was far from God.

There was no one in my life, not even my parents or his parents, who counseled me with Truth, talked to me about covenant or vows, or that GOD chose me to be the mother and I was needed and valued. No one. I have no idea if I would have listened, but it is shocking to me in retrospect that no one talked to me about those things. My mom just said that I sounded like I did when I was 15, and that she was afraid I would end up kidnapped and in Mexico in a brothel. I'm sure she said other things, but I don't remember them. The general sense of what I heard was "you're crazy."

Shortly after I left, my husband moved in with the female co-worker who I thought he was having an affair with, reinforcing my belief that he didn't really love me and that I didn't matter. He immediately filed for divorce and to have full custody. At the time, I believed they were all better off without me; I didn't matter and anyone could fill my spot.

The enemy came in strong, bound me and took me captive. I thought I was free, yet I was deceived in thinking freedom was in being alone and doing what I thought I wanted to do.

The Voice of the Siren Song

There is the voice of the siren song,
It woos us and seduces
To string us along

Into the place
Of the darkest night
Where there is no light
No spiritual sight

Believing the voices of the lying one
We turn to escape, to flee, to run
Into the arms of the one we think
Can save us, but brings us to the brink

Of the abyss of fools,
Swayed by the enemy's tools.

Yet God is still sovereign,
He comes for the lost
He paid the price,
The highest cost

And He is relentless
In drawing us home
We will yet see Him supreme
On the throne.

Dancing on the Edge of Reality
(Run Away Child, Run Away ~ Part Five)

This time in my life is a blur; I do not really remember the sequence of events very well, and am not sure how much was real or visions. I was seeing and hearing things all the time and having very strange experiences.

Once, I was fooling around with someone and went into his room where there was a full wall poster of who I knew had to be satan. I asked the man about it and he said, "Oh yeah, he's my bud. We talk all the time." I left. "Something" in me kept me from giving over to that! (Thank you, Father!) One day when I was in my rented room, some men and women came to the door to talk about God. They had Bibles. They looked at me, then each other, and said, "apostasy." I had no idea what that meant. Some years later, I heard the word, and remembered this occasion. I looked it up and found out that it means living without faith.

Another day I was walking somewhere and became doubled over in excruciating pain. I called my husband and asked him to take me to the hospital. I had an ovarian cyst that had ruptured, and the doctor said afterward that they weren't sure I was going to come back after the anesthesia. I remember thinking I didn't want to come back, and "heard" that I couldn't go yet because of my children. I believe now that the ovarian cyst rupturing was a judgment, resulting from lifestyle choices. I believe God was trying to get my attention because I wasn't listening any other way, although I was not aware of this at the time. My heart was completely walled off and the conflicting voices were so confusing that I was numb from paralysis.

I moved to a studio in North Park and got a job as a stripper; I wanted to live existentially, in the moment, with nothing mattering. I experienced date rape during this time, when I wasn't supposed to have sex because I was still healing from the ovarian cyst rupturing. Now I was spotting continually.

One day I was taking a bus somewhere and had an experience that I don't know to this day if it was real or a vision. A woman came onto the bus that a transparent, very loose black gown covering bones. Her eyes were empty. I "heard" that if I kept going the way I was, that would be me.

I joined a group that was called "Baby Angel Training." It was a metaphysical, experiential New Age group. One time we went to the Sierra Madre Mountain, in East San Diego County to "experience oneness with "mother earth." This was accomplished by all of us getting naked and rolling in the dirt, then giving each other massages of dirt. Another time the "guru" gave us all "new names." He said my name was Moriah, or Mariah (he didn't spell it). It is interesting to me that Mariah means bitterness or rebellion, and Moriah means chosen by Jehovah. Both are actually true — two sides of the same coin. God chooses each of us, creating our life for a purpose. We can embrace Him and His life, or we can turn in rebellion and become bitter. A very dear Christian friend once told me that he was surprised I hadn't turned bitter after my childhood experiences. Perhaps it is because I always knew that God isn't responsible for human choices. Anyway, back to the "guru." My short stint with this group ended when he told us at this meeting that he was to be called "LORD!" That was the end of that for me. I did have "something" inside me that knew he wasn't LORD.

All this happened within a timeframe of just a few months. God has His ways of getting our attention. I believe my mother and father were praying; my mom probably crying her eyes out. Her deepest fear was broken families and lost children. My life was spinning out of control and she was probably on her knees day and night. My dad, who I know loved me to the best of his ability, was angry with my husband, as he was supposed to "take care of me." I know that they had to be horribly fearful for my children as well.

As I think about my gifts and my journey, I am convinced that there are many who are in the New Age movement that are "seers." God Himself has given them the gift, but because there was no place for that gift in the traditional "church" (i.e. religion), they turned towards an avenue where their gift was accepted and could be developed. The devil always counterfeits and/or perverts what God intends for good.

Calling Your Name

Is your life shattered?
You thought nothing mattered?
Dreams dead in the dust;
No one you can trust?

The King of the Universe
Is calling your name
Do you hear Him?
You are not insane

His voice alone
Is the one that is true.
You are not abandoned;
He is coming for you!

Out of the Darkness, Into the Light

I have no explanation for what happened, except that my mother must have been praying. I had not been witnessed to, had not had someone recently preach to me, hadn't gone to church and had not had anyone share Christ with me. I was in my studio room and one minute was "normal," while in the next minute I had a life-changing experience. All I can do is describe what happened as my reality shifted:

SUDDENLY I became instantly aware of my sin(s). I believe that the Holy Spirit brought a spirit of repentance, because my perception of my life shifted. Immediately I knew that there was a God and that I was in complete sin before him, that I deserved to die. In fact, face to face with the reality of what I had done, how I had been living my life, I *wanted* to die. I was prostrate on the floor, weeping, begging God to let me die because the reality of having to live my life with what I had done was too painful; I could not bear it. I wept and cried out to God, begging Him to let me die for what seemed like hours. At some point I realized God was not going to let me die. From somewhere deep within me, I cried out, "Jesus, save me!"

The room became filled with light. My eyes were still closed as I lay prostrate on the floor, but I "saw" Jesus standing there. I saw His feet, His robe, though not His face, only brilliant white light. He touched my shoulder. I was instantly delivered from the demonic torment, healed of the issue of blood, and knew I was saved. Jesus was my savior, healer, and deliverer!

I called my mom right away and she said she would get a plane ticket and come out to help me. The next day I went to work and quit. I told my boss what happened. Jesus appeared to me and saved me, and I could not do this work anymore.

> *"Giving thanks unto the Father, which hath made us meet to be partakers of the inheritance of the saints in light; Who hath delivered us from the power of darkness, and hath translated us into the kingdom of his Son: In whom we have redemption through his blood, even the forgiveness of sins."* Colossians 1:12-14 (KJV)

Alive!

One moment in darkness
The next in light
Spiritually blind
New given sight
Bound and captive
Now set free
Alive in Christ eternally!

The Grace of God
(Now I Hear His Voice)

Oh, the immeasurable grace of God! My Mom came out immediately, and helped me get a lawyer. She tried to mediate with my husband and I, telling him how sorry I was and wanted to get back with him, and his response was, "Well, she should be sorry!" I agree, and knew that he was right not to want to be with me after what I had done. After all, I didn't really believe he loved me for who I was. How could he? I had no idea who I was, and one of the core beliefs I held was that I really didn't matter.

My mom found a lawyer and I met with him while she was here. My husband then got a lawyer also, and insisted that we both have psychological testing. My biggest fear was manifesting; now it would be "proven" that I was crazy. This became a very long, drawn-out process, but immediately I was able to have the girls over to visit. At night I would lay on the pull-out couch in my studio with them, with one in each arm, and that's how we would sleep. I was so thankful for every moment I had with them. I cherished them more than life. It's true that you don't realize what you have until it's gone. I knew I didn't deserve to have my husband back, but I was so thankful that I could have time with my children and was determined to do everything I could to love them and raise them to know they are loved.

My mom also helped me find a new job. I applied at the City of San Diego, but there was a long application process. After approximately six months, I was hired into their clerical pool. In the meantime, I was immediately hired at the University for Humanistic Studies. I found that God truly meets us right where we are. This university taught many New Age classes, and I was surrounded by men and women espousing the things that I had been indoctrinating myself with. As I heard them, the Spirit of God within me showed me the lies at the root of all of them. In fact, I would often doze off when they were talking about things that were false, then wake up at the moment truth came in. It is astonishing to me that they didn't counsel me for falling asleep during meetings; I know it was God's grace!

Once I went to the copy machine first thing in the morning and lifted the lid to place my paper down. There was already a paper there that "someone" must have left. It was a page of poems that were written from a victim mindset, "Oh woe is me; everyone is out to get me" type thinking. I was immediately convicted as I read them and realized how ridiculous it sounded.

Another time one of the professors who taught "Primal Screaming" told me that I needed to go outside and scream as loud as I could, that it would release pent-up anger and pain and I would be released from negativity. I did it. Hah! Everyone in the complex came running out to see who was being murdered! I was called in to the President's office and told that if I ever did anything like that again, I'd be fired on the spot!

The glorious grace of God began working in my life in a huge way. I got in at the City of San Diego and was able to move into a one-bedroom apartment, part of a four-plex, at the beach. I gave the girls the bedroom and slept on big floor pillows in the living room. God led me to a wonderful Assembly of God Church two blocks away, where I immediately felt part of the family of God in a way that I had never felt growing up. I was in the church whenever the doors were open – both morning services and Sunday school in between, Sunday night, and mid-week service. I joined women's groups, single's groups, and Bible Study groups, mid-week.

This church was a wonderful blend of good doctrine and an expression of the gifts, especially the Sunday night service. It was here that I saw people expressing prophetic words and visions they received. It was "normal" Christianity, but one that I had never seen or experienced before. My religious background did not include any of this, but it was all biblical. I had some incredible things happen here. I received a vision during one service where the Holy Spirit showed me a picture of a major stronghold, a perverse idol deeply rooted from childhood. I actually saw it, in the spirit, in me, and I saw it leave. As soon as He showed me it, it was broken. Immediately!

Another time He showed me a false teaching that I had received in my wandering years and exposed that as well – broken off! I am thankful that I was able to receive such solid teaching and wonderful church experiences in the early years of my Christian walk. I went back some years later and it was not the same experience at all. The church had suffered after one of the assistant pastor's left his wife and children for another woman (maybe the church secretary, although I'm not sure about that).

We were in the middle of a big custody battle, with mediators interviewing, counselors "observing" how we interacted with the kids playing, etc. It was a very trying time. I knew God was with me, but I was afraid of what would happen in court. One night, at the Sunday evening service, I joined a prayer circle by the altar. No one was laying hands on anyone, or leading the time of prayer. Each person was praying individually and the presence of God was very strong. I heard God say, "The psychologist will recommend that the father have custody," (I slumped to the floor in anguish) then I heard, "but it will be okay." I stood on that Word over the next few weeks, and it was as if I was transported into a cocoon of grace. I was aware of Him continually. I was living each moment very circumspectly, very conscious of His Holy Presence.

The day of court arrived. The judge noted that the Psychologist's report stated that both the plaintiff and the defendant had a lot of issues (she proceeded to read each of our negative traits), but that because the girls' father was remarried and in a home with a *family* (he had married the woman he moved in with and she had two older children), the girls would be better off with him. Then she said, "Nevertheless, I find that the parents will have joint legal custody, the mother having physical custody with the father having visitation rights." I was astonished. It was exactly as He had told me. "The king's heart is in the hand of the LORD, as the rivers of water: he turneth it whithersoever he will." (Proverbs 21:1 KJV)

During this time, the Lord became my Rock, my hope when all hope seemed gone. I learned that when He says something, it will absolutely be as He said. I have learned that this is a "Rhema" word, versus "Logos." Logos is the written word, as in the Bible and even Jesus, being the Logos, the Word made flesh. Rhema is a word that Holy Spirit illuminates for a specific time, or an utterance by the Holy Spirit for a situation. That's my paraphrase of both.

My daily prayer was that God would give me wisdom to raise my daughters. I felt I had no idea how to do that, and I certainly didn't want to raise my kids as I was raised. I am certain that God knew I would do that, and that is why He gave me favor with the judge. My ex-husband was gracious enough to put the girls into a Christian daycare near my house. I tried for a while to do a plant maintenance business. I had had a desire to own a plant nursery and thought that would be a good way to begin. I borrowed some money from my parents to start, "Laney's Plants Alive" and immediately got a few clients. The door-to-door of selling plants to businesses was too hard, and I didn't have much room to store them, but I got a few good clients for the maintenance function. When it was time for that door to close, the Lord led me to begin doing Christian daycare. I had already started watching one little girl to supplement the plant business. God provided when there was a need!

As part of the overall property where I lived, there was a large, two-bedroom house with a huge, fenced-in backyard on the same lot. When it became available, I approached the landlord and convinced him that it would work for me to do daycare, although at the time I didn't even have one child lined up yet to watch! I had no money for a deposit, so he let me "pay for it" by helping clean and fix up the new house and the one I was moving from! The favor and grace of God! Now I see it was all part of His hand moving in my life to bring me forward into His plan.

After about two years of doing daycare, when Cara was in 2nd grade and Sara in kindergarten, I couldn't do it anymore; it was too taxing emotionally and physically. At the right time, I was blessed with a great job at the City of San Diego. I started in the Clerical Pool, where I got the opportunity to experience a number of different departments within the City government.

One of those assignments was at the Park and Recreation Department's, Coastline Parks Division. This turned into a full-time permanent position and I worked there for ten years. It was a wonderful blessing. The woman who initially hired me and was my immediate supervisor was a Christian with the same name as my mother and also had five children! There were other Christians there too, and I made some wonderful friends there and received a lot of emotional support. God was moving mightily in my life. Some of the amazing things that happened during that time:

I took Cara to the doctor because her heartbeat was erratic. The doctor did an X-ray and said she had mitral valve prolapse. I was so afraid. I didn't know what to do. I sought God in prayer, for what seemed like hours, and I had a vision of Cara being on an elevated table, and surrounded by five men in robes who seemed to be doing something to her. After a while, they were finished.

I knew she was healed. I took her back to the doctor for another x-ray, and her heart was fine!

A friend of a friend needed a place to stay, so I let him. He was very sick. He said he had brain cancer. I told him God could heal him, and shared my testimony, and Cara's. He said he didn't believe in God. I told him that I thought God was trying to get his attention, and to start reading the Bible and turn to Him. I found out later from my friend that he eventually turned to the Lord and was saved and healed!

The reality is that the very power that sets us free provides power for the hearer, who is listening with a heart of faith. When I hear of the testimony of another, the same anointing that provided the miracle is available for me, if I hear with a heart of faith and believe. God is not a respecter of persons. In other words, His Word is true and we can stand upon it and believe to receive the manifestation of that Word. It also means that what God does for one He will do for another, because of the blood of Christ that was shed. The blood of the Lamb was shed for all. If we believe in our heart that we were sinners and that Christ died for our sins, we can receive forgiveness. His perfect, sinless life is atonement for our sins. He takes our sins and provides His life for ours! In the same way, if we hear that Jesus heals, and believe, we can receive healing also! How powerful is God's love for us!

I had an experience that gave me a glimpse into the way that God could use a yielded vessel. I was at a PTA meeting and they were doing a presentation on Child Abuse. This was in the early 1980's when it became mandatory for those, other than physicians, to report when there was suspicion children were being abused. After the presentation was a question and answer period. A very large African-American man stood up and said, "What I do in my own home is my own business and I'll do what I damn well please to my children."

I felt something rise up inside me, an anger with such white-hot passion that I was shocked. I was compelled to speak, but my mind was arguing against it. Over the course of some minutes, the fire inside became so hot that something within me propelled me up out of my seat and I said, "Those children are not *yours*, they are a gift from God and you will be held accountable to Him for how they are treated and raised." I continued for a few more minutes along those lines, then sat down, shaking, and shocked. The room was completely still, not a sound made by anyone and no one moving. After a few minutes the PTA President said, "Meeting adjourned."

God brought supernatural provision! Once when I was low on food, people showed up at my door with food! He also provided a wonderful friend, a new neighbor who was a believer and had two small girls the same ages as mine! They became the best of friends, too. Oh my, did we have an awesome time together! We were constantly together, reading the Word, taking day trips to the mountains, fellowshipping and having a great time.

Once we had angelic intervention. We were at "Garbage Beach" at the end of Sunset Cliffs, in Point Loma, which you get to by going down a big flight of stairs, then walking over a field of boulders. When we were coming back, a huge wave came up over us out of nowhere. The surf was at least 20 feet beyond where we were, and this rogue wave overtook us. The kids were screaming, we were sliding on the now wet rocks. Out of nowhere, two men appeared in scuba gear, picked up the kids (two each, using both arms) and carried them to safety. After we got there, we turned to thank them, and they were nowhere in sight! Once again, God was my deliverer; sending angels over me, my friend and our kids.

I began teaching Sunday School at the church and formed a Children's choir. During this time Cara received Jesus into her heart. Everything was going great. In hindsight, I know that when everything is going great, it is time to be on guard!

Always with You

Though guilt and shame
Clouded your eyes
I never let you go.

Your heart could not yet realize
The depths to which
My love would flow
Even to the pit below.
I was always with you
Though you didn't know.

Into the Wilderness
(Through the Doors of Offense and Impatience)

Then some things happened and my life took another turn. I was involved in Singles ministry and we would meet in various homes. One evening we were meeting in the home of one of the leaders and she told us to get our drinks out of the refrigerator. When I opened the refrigerator door, I saw that there was alcohol. I was very surprised about that.

Another time, at another home, a couple that were recently married shared how they met. The woman said, "I'd been single for eight years." Inside, I heard a voice, "That's too long; I can't wait that long."

During this time, my best friend began dating someone in leadership at the church. She got pregnant and had an abortion. Nothing happened to the man; his life went on as usual. She stopped attending church and slipped away from the Lord and our friendship. I was so angry at God that He let all that happen.

I was offended at the leadership in the church. In retrospect, I see that I had a choice, to humble myself and trust God or be bitter and turn away. Ps. 119:165 states, "Great peace have they which love thy law and nothing shall offend them." Becoming offended will sideline you, taking you out of God's will and plan. It is a form of pride; we are in effect saying to ourselves that we know better than God. John Bevere wrote a book about it entitled, "The Bait of Satan," in which he describes how satan uses offense to snare and entrap us.

Then I met my second husband. He said he was a Christian, but he smoked cigarettes and pot, and drank. I had guilt from judging my first husband for his weaknesses, and how that influenced my leaving him. I felt deep down that true love would have stuck with him through his struggle. I also was still struggling with inferiority, made worse by my first husband's rejection, although it was certainly justified by my actions at the time.

Here was a chance to help someone. He'd had a bad divorce and couldn't see his daughter. Hello; red flag! I really thought "my love" would save him. He was very expressive emotionally, which was refreshing to me. He was also very engaging and involved with the girls; in fact, we co-led a Girl Scout Troop for two years after we were married. He had a big heart, but was also very wounded from severe mental and physical childhood abuse. He had fits of anger, towards others, before we were married; I never thought it would be turned on me.

At a pivotal moment in our relationship, when I had a choice that would take it to a more physical level, the phone rang. I went to answer it, and when I picked it up there was no one there. I "knew" it was a way out of the situation (God always provides a way out of temptation). I didn't make the right choice.

After we married, I eventually started smoking cigarettes again, and drinking, thinking I could "show him" that we could quit together. Unfortunately, he had no desire to quit. I smoked pot again – one time – because I wanted to show him that you could do it and not "have" to keep doing it. Well, I was in for a big surprise. After I smoked it, immediately I was overwhelmed with a multitude of voices – a cacophony of chatter. I felt nauseous and dizzy. I went into the bathroom and threw up, repenting whole-heartedly to God for my choice.

Over time his "emotional expressiveness" turned abusive. I tolerated the abuse toward me, probably because deep down I believed I deserved it. When his abuse turned to the kids… that was the end of the marriage for me. I had to be very strategic in planning how to get out of it, because he was very vindictive and plotted revenge towards those that hurt him. After a few months of carefully laying the groundwork, we separated, then I filed for divorce.

In the Bible, the word for "sorcery" is pharmacopeia – it means drugs. There is a reality that drugs are a gateway to the forces of wickedness in heavenly places, i.e. the demonic. You may have a hard time believing this, especially if you like to smoke pot or even cigarettes. I bring up cigarettes because one of the times I quit (not the final time) I noticed my mind speeding up after the nicotine kicked in, and I liked the extra "mental activity" I had. Now, it may well have not been the mental stimulant and it was my own voice, but the reality is that it hindered my hearing Holy Spirit, because He has a still, small voice. Like it or not, nicotine is a drug!

God had already told me years before to quit smoking, when I was in the custody battle. This time, it was much harder. I tried many ways and many times to break the habit. I was lying and hiding it from my kids. Sara followed me secretly one time and confronted me, and I flat-out lied about it. She pointed out the lit ashes on the ground. I was mortified that I was so addicted I would lie to her! That was the final straw for me.

During this time of my life, Sara was having anxiety about my dying, and frequent stomach pain. There were no words I could give her to ease the fears. I wasn't walking with the Lord, so I could not comfort her about eternity as I didn't have assurance myself. The doctor said she was pre-ulcerous. I was having nightmares about end-of-the-world scenarios – tidal waves, earthquakes. Looking back, it is clear that the Lord was trying to get my attention. Sara is sensitive spiritually (discerning) although I didn't know that then, nor what that meant. She probably was sensing my spiritual state and the atmosphere in our home was not "filled with the Holy Spirit."

I had a friend at work who saw my backsliding and asked me one day – "Do you ever wonder about what would happen if the Lord chose to return today?" Now, only God knows who will be saved, whereas there is much discussion among Christians about whether when you are once saved you are always saved, or if you can lose your salvation. I am rather pragmatic in my thinking - why take a chance? My conscience was pricked, and I was plagued with guilt and condemnation. I knew what the Word of God says about backsliding, and it wasn't good.

> "For if after they have escaped the pollutions of the world through the knowledge of the Lord and Savior Jesus Christ, they are again entangled therein, and overcome, the latter end is worse with them than the beginning. For it had been better for them not to have known the way of righteousness, than, after they have known it, to turn from the holy commandment delivered unto them. But it is happened unto them according to the true proverb, The dog is turned to his own vomit again; and the sow that was washed to her wallowing in the mire." 2 Peter 2:20-22 (KJV)

Now I was in a bad state. I was too embarrassed to go to church again; I believed the devil's lie that I had done the unforgiveable because I backslid.

Also, when I was divorced the first time, I wasn't a Christian, but the second time I was. I believed that because I divorced as a Christian, I couldn't come back to Him now. This led to depression.

I began attending CODA (Co-Dependents Anonymous) meetings for help, because I saw how my wanting to "help" and "save" someone was dysfunctional. In fact, I really saw how my whole family structure growing up was very co-dependent. This was my first introduction to the 12 Steps. I now began seeing how the early sexual molestation had affected my identity and behaviors, so I began going to SLAA (Sex and Love Addicts Anonymous) meetings also. I was learning about healing the "inner child" and believed that these core issues had a lot to do with my backsliding. I also saw a psychologist and got on Prozac for a period of time.

The last year of my stint at the Parks and Recreation Department, I began going to San Diego City College, with the desire to become a Chemical Dependency Counselor. I had seen firsthand (more than once now) the devastating effects of drugs and alcohol in a person's life, and people had always been able to open up to me about their problems. In fact, co-workers were often telling me I should be a counselor, so it seemed a natural fit.

I hated clerical work; I always had. I got into it because my mother suggested I take typing in high school, as I could "always get a job typing," which was true. I had tried other types of work (sales, waitressing) and didn't like those either. I really didn't know what I wanted to do with my life and had no idea what my gifts were. I always got excellent grades in English, and was a good writer, but didn't really know what to do with that. I didn't feel "called" to anything. I wasn't one of those who always knew what they wanted to do in life, in fact, I never gave it any thought as a child.

Timing worked out for me in this situation. The City was trying new flexibility programs for their employees. I was one of the first to apply for, and get approved for telecommuting. Back in those days, there was a computer program called "Carbon Copy" which allowed remote access to the work computer files from home. I was able to work whatever hours were best for me, as long as the work got done by the deadlines. This was perfect as I could be there when the girls got home from school.

I reduced my hours to 75%, and was going to school full-time, doing my work from home. The next year, it was decided because of budget cuts, that they were eliminating a position and they needed a full-time person in the office, so I had to make a choice. I chose to quit and finish school. I applied for financial aid and scholarships (receiving both), and supplemented these by doing word processing from home for other students.

Over the course of the next year, I received all the credits necessary to become a Drug Counselor, but the pay was such that I was making a lot more money doing clerical work! I was a single mom, so I had to make a wise decision and money was a huge factor. I was considering going on to become a Psychologist instead, but God began drawing me back to Him *through* the Psychology and Philosophy classes, believe it or not. As we discussed and debated different theories and beliefs, I realized that what I knew, beyond a shadow of a doubt, was that Jesus was the only way to bring real change in a person's life. Theories are just that, and behavior modification techniques are helpful to change behaviors, but they don't change the person's heart or heal the deepest wounds that caused the behavior needing change.

During this time, I also became involved with a man that was in Alcoholics Anonymous. I was still drinking occasionally, as I didn't think I had a problem with alcohol; I didn't drink every day, only when the kids went to be with their dad every other weekend. I began going to AA to be a support to him, and learned that I really did have a problem with alcohol, because it was what I turned to in my loneliness.

This man was a sexual deviant, (I met him at Black's Beach so that should have been a clue) and God used this relationship to break me of my dependence on sex and relationships for self-worth and value. It was a horribly addictive relationship on both of our parts, and we both knew it was very unhealthy and felt helpless to stop. The girls couldn't stand him, (they sensed his perversity, I'm sure), and I was obsessed to be with him.

My children were naturally affected by my backsliding. I had made the mistake of no longer attending church after divorcing my second husband, believing I'd done the unforgiveable. Also, they were at an age that it seemed they didn't "need" me as much, so I became self-absorbed in searching for my own happiness. Their dad was on his third marriage, and that was also affecting the girls (now teenagers). My youngest was sneaking around, getting in with the wrong crowd. In fact, the very day that I first met the deviant at Black's Beach, is the first time this manifested in a very obvious way. Unfortunately, I did not see the correlation between my behavior and what was happening with my children. If I knew then what I know now! This escalated, naturally, and I didn't have a clue how to fix it. I read her diary once and she had written some things that were alarming, so I talked to her dad and her best friend. Cara was also very disturbed at what Sara was involved in. We did an "intervention" so to speak. This didn't help; in fact, it got worse.

I ended up going to a Psychologist again because of some of the things I did during the perverted relationship that caused me to have such guilt and shame that I was crying and could not stop. I went on Prozac once again, for a period of time.

As I quit drinking, and became more "present." I was working to gain control over the girls again. It was a hard row now that they were teenagers. They had seen me backslide and deep down probably thought religion was all a hoax. They told me they liked it better when I was drinking because they could do what they wanted. I knew what that was like; I recalled being a teenager and our group of friends were always wanting to go to the house of the kid who had a single mom who drank, because we could get away with everything.

Sara continued to act out and she went to live at her dad's. We were hoping that would work, but it didn't. I was so afraid, and so hopeless. I went to another Psychologist, getting on Prozac again because I was so afraid and worried I could not think straight. I needed coping tools and to quiet my mind. She was very kind, and said something so profound that it made a major shift in how I viewed myself. She said, "If your girls came to you and said they were doing some of the things that you have been doing, what would you do?" I said I would be appalled and heartbroken and do all I could to stop them. She said, "No one did that for you when you were a child, but now you are an adult and you have to be the one who takes care of the little girl within you."

At Christmas break, when I was off school and the kids were at their dad's for a week, I severed the perverted relationship. I spent nearly five full days in bed crying, getting to the point where I was so disgusted with my moping and self-pity that I literally screamed, "God, I am so lonely; please heal me!"

Immediately, the loneliness was lifted off of me. I was shocked! I always thought that emotions were something we have to deal with on our own. Certainly, we have to practice self-control, but I have found that if there is an emotional wound that is causing great manifestation and dysfunction in our lives, God wants to heal that core wound. My sexual "addiction" was caused by my needing love and attention so badly.

Unending Grace

The devil led me into bondage again
Intending to destroy my life through sin
But God in His love, never let go
His ways He would begin to show
Even when I turned from Him
He made a way for me to come back in
Even in my perverse state
He showed me it was never too late
His mercy and love are never ending
His grace enfolds the sheep He is tending
Ever teaching, always mending
Never losing sight of the purpose in His sending

The Voice Of Redemption

I turned my life completely to the Lord at this point. Before, I had been saved, healed, and delivered from demons, but I thought that I had to take the new life that God had given me and make something great out of it on my own! I began going back to church, praying a lot, and really seeking Him like I hadn't since I was first born-again.

I told God that I didn't care if I never had another relationship again, but that if it was in His will for my life. My only desire was to have a Godly marriage, so my kids could see how it was supposed to be. They weren't seeing it in the world, and hadn't seen it in my life or their dad's, and I knew it was possible. There had been a wonderful, Godly couple in my early born-again time who had watched my girls one weekend when I went to a singles ministry camp. When I walked into their house, the presence of God was so strong I knew I wanted that. I had never forgotten that experience and knew that there was a way to have a Godly marriage. There were people who were doing it, even though I hadn't seen it modeled myself.

I reached out to the pastor for help with Sara. After I explained all the problems I was having with her, he said, "Well, what have you been doing in your life up to this point?" I told him some of it, and he said, "Well, what do you expect?" I broke at that point, weeping in godly sorrow and shame, knowing that he was right and that I was responsible for much of her pain and actions. After I acknowledged this, he offered help.

I was still going to AA meetings and met a man named Kerry at one of them. It was suggested to him to talk to me to see if I could help him with his resume, which I did. It wasn't for another few months, though, at another meeting, that we really began talking. He worked nights and I worked days, so we rarely had a lot of time to spend together. We would go for walks at the beach and talk.

Kerry had had a powerful born-again experience at 19, and a few solid years of Christian growth with some strong fundamental, fervent Apostolic/Prophetic teachers, even going to Bible College in England. However, he hadn't fully broken it off with a girl he'd been dating before getting saved.

That began his descent into backsliding for 20 years. Even though he did break up with her within a year, he had begun smoking pot and drinking again and didn't stop those habits. So, when I met him he had a similar story of having started out strong, falling into temptation and subsequent "lost" years. We were both hungry for the deeper things of God, and had many other things in common.

Christmas night of 1993, the girls were at their Dad's. He was bringing them back the next morning for our trip to Maryland to visit my family. Kerry and I went to a coffeehouse in Ocean Beach. We were having an intense time of fellowship and came back to my house to get into the Word. I had two very old antique Bibles I wanted to show him. We each had one, and were sharing from the Scriptures with each other. The Holy Spirit was so present in our midst — the atmosphere was thick with the Glory of God! I had a vision of us ministering together and I knew we would be married, that this was God's purpose in our relationship. Later in our lives, I would find out that there is a process to a vision becoming reality.

I was flying high in the Spirit as we went to Maryland the next day. I tried to tell the girls about it, but they weren't interested as they'd heard me talk many, many times about how great a new relationship was. As they got to know Kerry, it was amazing to me how they immediately respected him. He was so kind, and gentle, so "real" that Sara told me, "You better not hurt him!" It was interesting to me that she was so observant of my callous interactions with men. Of course, it was from my wounded-ness and not wanting to be hurt myself that I hurt others first, but to her it looked as if I was just very hard, bitter, and calloused.

A few months later, Kerry proposed and we began planning our marriage. It was a very stressful time for me. I was going to school full-time and working out of the home. The girls were teenagers and still walking out the result of my backsliding by acting out in the ways they had grown accustomed to.

There was a time when Kerry and I had one of the very few fights we'd ever had. Kerry was honestly saying that he didn't know if he could handle having two teenagers. I overreacted in pain, hurt that he wasn't "man enough" (in my eyes) to love my kids as much as I did. I hated him at that moment, and told God that if He wanted me to marry him, He'd have to change my feelings, because I never wanted to see Kerry or talk to him again. Immediately the feelings left. It was an additional confirmation to me that God's hand was in this relationship and we were to be married.

Turnaround

Though we walk in darkness,
Choosing the way of sin
His love is ever present,
His goodness brings us back to Him.

He shines his light upon our ways
His Truth reveals the price we paid
And the results in our lives
From the path we laid.

His mercy pours out on us in grace
Enabling us to seek His face
We turn around to walk with Him
Into divine purpose we enter in.

Turning Point
(The Baptism of the Holy Ghost Testifies of Power)

One day when I was on the campus of City College, between classes, I was so burdened for Sara that I was crying out to God. I was unable to concentrate on classes, on anything, obsessed with fear about what would happen to her. I had no idea what to do, how to reach her. She was running away, doing drugs, angry with me and rebelling against all rules. I was weeping and praying, not caring who saw me as I walked in the depths of depression and anxiety. From out of nowhere, as I was crying out, another language came out of my mouth! I was praying in tongues! I had heard others do it at churches I'd attended, but had not received it myself. I was astonished, but more importantly, I had the "knowing" in my spirit that Sara was going to be okay.

When Kerry and I walked later that day, a butterfly flew in front of me as we walked on the beach and I shared what had happened earlier. This was confirmation to me of transformation. Then Kerry told me that he had also received the baptism of the Holy Ghost that day! Amazing, in two different locations, on the same day, we received! Later that evening, a close friend told me that she had been praying for Sara and when she looked up, Sara's name was in the clouds. More confirmation.

Power of Change

The enemy speaks
Bringing fear to our soul.
Holy Spirit speaks
His love makes us whole.
The enemy brings
Foreboding and dread.
Hope comes when we look to Christ
As the Head.
He is before all things,
By Him they consist,

And in His name,
We have the power to resist
All the devil's threats and lies
For we know that,
To God, there is no surprise
He is well aware
Of what we are facing
He brings hope and faith
For our embracing.
As we trust in Him,
He will show us the way.
Transforming power comes
As we pray!

Divine Strategies

The Holy Spirit began speaking to me of His strategy for Sara, to move her away from the bad influences. He kept highlighting Jude 23 to me, "And others save with fear, pulling them out of the fire..." Even so, it was a hard decision to make. I loved the beach, but it had become a place of fear and foreboding for me, with all that was happening with Sara and the memories of my own backsliding.

We were attending a very good church in Escondido, where Kerry really liked the teaching, and decided that it was far enough away to keep Sara away from the bad influences, but close enough to Cara and her Dad. I was finished with school except for a few classes which I would take in the fall, and was working part-time, enabling me to spend more time with her.

We found a three-bedroom house to rent in Escondido, and moved in after our honeymoon. I found a great counselor for Sara, a street-wise young black woman who Sara immediately related to. I got her enrolled in homeschooling and we began the hard work of learning to relate again. We were once so close, the Holy Spirit reminded me, and those bonds were not easily broken.

I had some difficult choices to make. It was hard to make it on Kerry's salary plus my part-time job. After a period of time, I began looking for full-time work. On the morning of an interview for a really great job, Sara said that she felt like she was going to "do something." I was torn. Was she acting out, manipulating me, or was this real? I decided to forgo the interview. I really felt it was the best choice. Sara needed my full attention at this time, and it was the first time in my life that I actually felt empowered to give her what she needed. When she was young, her neediness was very hard and I didn't have it in me to give. I determined that I was going to do it, and it was one of the best decisions I ever made.

Meanwhile, Cara was facing some life issues because of a situation at her dad's house and decided to move in with us in Escondido while she finished her senior year of high school. That was also a challenging time for all of us, but mostly for Cara. Going through emotional pain, and the reality of having to drive back and forth from Escondido to Point Loma every day for the rest of the year, Cara found out that she was a lot stronger than she thought she was. I was becoming very proud of both my girls for the hard decisions they had to make and their choices that made them stronger and wiser.

We were all learning to adjust to this new family structure and dynamics, as well as location. We were all growing. Kerry was very reclusive and distant from years of bachelorhood, and it was beautiful to see how God was using all of our brokenness to bring love into Kerry's life also. The girls respected and loved Kerry, and he was so gentle and kind, and "real" with them. They began to see how real relating between a man and a woman looks like, communicating hard things in love. Oh, at first, it was the usual dysfunctional coping behaviors (Kerry going off by himself to be alone and my storming off into the car), but that was short-lived. We wouldn't allow Kerry to withdraw, lovingly drawing him in to our spaces, and my storming off didn't produce the results I wanted, so I stopped!

> *"God setteth the solitary in families: he bringeth out those which*
> *are bound with chains: but the rebellious dwell in a dry land."*
> *Psalms 68:6 (KJV)*

Turn and Keep on Turning

Turn and keep on turning to me
I know what you need to be set free
My purpose for your life will stand
I desire that you take the land
That was given into the enemy's hand.

You and your children and those to come
Will no longer be under satan's thumb
You are mine and mine alone
Let Me be King on your heart's throne.

I have a plan and it is for your best
Do not turn away and settle for less
Turn and keep on turning to me
I will give you divine strategy.

All that you need is found in Me.

Hopelessness and the Power of a Rhema Word

After we were married a few years, I became depressed again. I starting having thoughts of worthlessness and guilt and regrets about my past come back, even though things were going well in many ways.

Now I "knew" that there was no hope. I was now trying to walk the Christian walk, with a Godly man, doing all the "right" things, and depression returned; therefore, it was hopeless. I believed it would be recurring for the rest of my life. Now I was *really* depressed!

What is hopelessness? Thinking things will never change. Many things can cause depression, but hopelessness comes from not truly knowing the power of God and/or not believing He can change things.

The voice of hopelessness can come from substance abuse or other addictive lifestyles. When you live in a state of addiction, you are consumed with your next "fix" and it establishes a lifestyle of havoc. During those chaotic times you are not truly present, so things pile up and catastrophes happen (which God uses to try and get your attention).   Now there is a big mess to constantly deal with, there is never enough time to catch up and fix it all, and you don't have the skills or coping tools to deal with it. Maybe that's actually the chicken/egg dilemma – you drank, used substances or other things (or people) to cope with the lack of tools to live life. Then, over the course of time, hopelessness sets in.

Of course, hopelessness can come from other things...a broken childhood, abuse at a young age and being powerless, those entrusted to your care not able to provide the love and nurturing necessary for your emotional well-being. When these things happen you live in a state of hopelessness as it seems there is no one that cares about what you think or feel.

Unfortunately, what usually happens (I assume there are exceptions) is that the cycles continue throughout our lives. We believe we are not worthy of love because we believe our parents didn't love us. We create similar situations in our lives because that is what we know and who we think we are, or what we deserve. Nothing changes until someone or something breaks that deserve

Nothing changes until someone or something breaks that pattern, such as divine intervention or a glimpse of something better that sparks a hunger in us that drives us to seek ways to change.

The voice of hopelessness in my life started with childhood sexual abuse and emotional abuse, leading to a rejection of my religion and moral upbringing through rebellion. I tried to escape the feelings with drugs, alcohol and many wrong choices. Even though I had a powerful salvation experience and strong walk of faith, offense sent me backwards for some years. My lifestyle was an abuse to myself, which also affected my children and led to two failed marriages. The second marriage was abusive because I subconsciously believed I deserved punishment. All of this set the stage for cyclical depression. It would be set off, triggered, by a memory of previous pain or failing.

Even after marrying Kerry, trying to do all the "right" things; going to church, living "for God," etc., the pattern continued. Now it seemed the cycles of depression would continue forever, and I felt truly hopeless. So one day in church, there I was, in a very dark place in my head. I have no idea what the pastor was speaking on; I was just in my head in a dark place, but crying out to God in my heart. Then there appeared a pinprick of light. I heard, "Your only hope is to get my Word inside you." I knew that was God, and immediately I had hope. God said so! There was hope! Get into His Word!

I began a daily committed time with Him in the Word. I had been doing devotionals daily, that started in the 12 step programs of AA, CODA, SLAA, and often there was a Bible verse associated with the devotional, but this was different. Now I was diligently, purposefully, seeking God through His Word. He began speaking to *me*, personally, through the Word. Holy Spirit was making the scriptures live as they hadn't in a long time. He began revealing Jesus to me, aspects of His divinity, and the realms of possibility in the Eternal Now.

After about six months, I realized I had not been depressed since that day God spoke to me, and I haven't since! Oh, I have days of being down, negative, but not *depressed* in that cyclical pattern of continual bombardment of memories that *prove I'm a failure*. No, the Word of God began living in me; Holy Spirit began reminding me of scriptures whenever a negative thought popped into my head! He was counseling me! He is the Counselor with a capital C! The supreme Counselor! Jesus is the great Physician, of all parts of our being!

> *"Now the God of hope fill you with all joy and peace in believing, that ye may abound in hope, through the power of the Holy Ghost."* Romans 15:13 (KJV)

Remember I said that when I was in that place of despair, my heart was crying out to God?

> *"Behold, the eye of the LORD is upon them that fear him, upon them that hope in his mercy; Let thy mercy, O LORD, be upon us, according as we hope in thee."* Psalms 33:18; 32 (KJV)

> *"For in thee, O LORD, do I hope: thou wilt hear, O Lord my God."* Psalms 38:15 (KJV)

> *"And now, Lord, what wait I for? My hope is in thee."* Psalms 39:7 (KJV)

> *"Why art thou cast down, O my soul? and why art thou disquieted in me? hope thou in God: for I shall yet praise him for the help of his countenance."* Psalms 42:5 (KJV)

He is the God of hope. He is our hope. He hears our cries. He has shown me that His mercy has always been with me, He has always poured out His mercy upon me when I cried out to Him. He is faithful to His covenant, and speaks His word to our hearts in power!

The Word of God

The word of God is alive, full of power
Overriding the enemy's tools to devour
God's word brings life to the depths of the soul
To restore us and to make us whole
The Word exposes the lies with His light
Where we were blind, He brings His sight
Leading us out from the soul's darkest night
Into a new day, hope dawning bright

As the Word became alive to me, my spirit was overflowing with revelation and I began flowing in poetry as never before. Jesus was being revealed to me in many aspects of His being that I had never known; Holy Spirit was illuminating the scriptures with the Presence of God and poems were the release of all that He was pouring into me.

We were living in Fallbrook now, and I was working part-time at the City of Vista. The girls were adults, going to college and living on their own. This gave me the blessing of time to spend in the Word as I had never had before.

God gave me two specific Rhema words during this time of intense study: Proverbs 18:16, "A man's gift makes room for him and brings him before great men," and Ps. 31:15, "My times are in your hands." At the time, I thought it must be about the poems.

It's Time!

One night, I was awakened by a voice; I heard clearly, "It's time!" It was an audible voice. I was immediately overcome by fear. Kerry was asleep; it was about 2:00 in the morning and I didn't want to wake him. I was questioning, "Who are you?" "Is this God or Satan?" I lay there for hours, seeking the Lord and asking for wisdom. What does that mean, "It's time?" "Time for what?" Towards dawn I was fairly certain that the Lord was telling me that my children were grown now, so that part of my life's purpose was finished, and that if I didn't start living for Him, I'd be out of here, my time would be up. It was time to fulfill my purpose in Christ. I really questioned whether or not I was hearing accurately, but felt I was. I lay there in a state of reverential fear, not knowing what it was I was supposed to do to live for Him more than I already was.

As dawn broke, the phone rang. It was Cara, crying hysterically. Fear gripped my soul. Cara is the "rational" daughter; very rarely did she have any kind of emotional outburst, and even more rarely did I "witness" her crying. Sara is the emotional daughter. "Mom," she sobbed, "I had a horrible nightmare. I dreamed that you told me you were dying. I begged you, 'No, Mom, I'm not ready for that, I need you, you can't die yet.' And you replied, 'It's time.'"

This was, obviously, confirmation to me that it *was* God I heard, and that He meant business. Now began the seeking to find out what it was He wanted me to do. I didn't really get any clear direction, so in my own understanding I began taking every opportunity to "live for Him." I began witnessing at work and praying for people, both things that were way out of my comfort zone. I didn't mind doing those things outside of work, but the whole, "Separation of church and state" mentality, was deeply ingrained in me from years of public service, plus the "You're crazy" voice that was still deep down inside me. No one at work knew my history, so I didn't have the "Who is going to listen to you with your past?" taunting voice nag me when I shared the Word of God in the workplace. However, it spoke loudly when I had an opportunity to share my testimony of salvation with people I interacted with on a daily basis.

It's Time!

The time is coming,
And now is,
For the world to know
That you are His.

His love must be shown,
His power made known,
That He would be seen
Upon your heart's throne,

His will having become
Your own.

Learning Authority

While I was working as a clerical employee for a governmental agency, God taught me about submission to authority. It was very interesting how God chose to teach me, and who the people He chose to use for my instruction. I had an agnostic boss who I thought was lazy and just putting in time until retirement. He would sit in his office and play computer games. There were piles of papers everywhere, I mean stacks and stacks of things on his desk, on the floor, on chairs, throughout the office, and they didn't seem to have any order to them. I came to that conclusion when he was frantically searching for a letter. He would pick up half a pile of one stack, look through it then place it on top of another stack.

I eventually went through it all and created a system to log in correspondence, the response and date of response, and a filing system as well. I felt sorry for my boss. He had a family member that had been given an early death sentence from birth due to a congenital disorder. I often wondered if perhaps he was depressed rather than lazy, and God put His compassion in me towards my boss. Holy Spirit reminded me that I was to respect the position he was in, and the education and life experience he had that raised him up to that position.

The other people I reported to in the office were equally "not deserving of my respect" in my opinion. One of my co-workers was a non-practicing Catholic with a big ego who bragged that he was just putting in time until retirement. Another was a very passive woman of the Baha'i faith, which is (my take on it from how she explained it to me) a conglomeration of a number of religions, all "works" oriented. There were a few others that worked there that all seemed to be just putting in time until retirement and doing the least amount of work possible. The "macho man" was constantly giving me last-minute things to do and it seemed to me that it was on purpose. In fact, I thought he had it in for me because he was "jealous" of my ability to get things done in a timely manner and with excellence.

So, circumstances kept creating this opportunity to serve him without offense or to get offended. God brought this to a head one day and I blew up at the man, yelling that he was deliberately giving me things late and trying to set me up to fail. He looked at me and said, "I feel the same way." I broke, humiliated and ashamed that I could have been so blind. I apologized profusely, over and over again, and made him cookies that night. Holy Spirit showed me how wrong I could be in my own understanding and how one lie can bring a false perception. This was freeing to me, as Holy Spirit continues to remind me when I have a blind spot in a relationship.

Lord of All

I raise up and I bring low,
I know what is needed for you to grow
Into the fullness of your calling.
My Spirit searches, always drawing,
Purging what will bring forth strife,
Desiring purity of heart in your life.

When you see Me as Lord of all,
There is nothing that can make you fall.

I began seeing spiritual battles raging over the kids. Sara had begun going in the wrong direction again. I even saw a spirit of death over her at one time when she came over. I also sensed that Cara was deeply struggling — she was shutting down, wouldn't talk. I didn't know anything about spiritual warfare at that time, and the church we were going to didn't teach it. This was before the internet, so I couldn't "google" it. God led me to fast and pray. On the fifth day of my fasting and praying, Sara came up to visit unannounced. She was very subdued. She shared something that was going on in her life. I saw repeating cycles from my life and I was so scared. Internally, as I was listening, I was crying out to God for help, telling Him that I had no idea what to say, but that I didn't want her repeating my mistakes.

After she finished telling me what was going on, I shared with her my experience of who Jesus is and what He had done in my life. The whole time I was telling her, I was listening closely waiting for the leading of Holy Spirit. Sara was extremely quiet, not normal for her, her head was down and she was listening, but I could not see any expression to know if I'd had an impact. She left and I had no idea if she had received or rejected what I said. The next morning, she called me, and told me that she had received Jesus into her heart and knew that it didn't matter if she was alone, if her Dad left her, if her boyfriend left her, it wouldn't matter, because she would never be alone again. Follow the Holy Spirit's lead! At that time in my life, had I not been fasting, I would have probably counseled from a self-righteous attitude. God knows what we need and how to get us in the place of humility where He can speak through us in love as a meek, yielded vessel. I loved my children intensely, but pride can cause a rift in the way words are spoken and received.

> *"And the servant of the Lord must not strive; but be gentle unto all men, apt to teach, patient, In meekness instructing those that oppose themselves; if God peradventure will give them repentance to the acknowledging of the truth; And that they may recover themselves out of the snare of the devil, who are taken captive by him at his will."* 2 Timothy 2:24-26 (KJV)

A Mother's Heart

A mother's heart is not at rest
Until she knows her children are blessed,
Walking in His truth and love
Secure in the salvation of God above.

Kerry and I had attended various churches in Fallbrook and none seemed the right fit for both of us. We found a Word of Faith church in another city that we both liked and wanted to attend. We were blessed to receive great teachings and the spiritual atmosphere was rich. An internationally known worship leader/teacher was the Worship Pastor. We learned much about worship through his teachings, and I was blessed to be on the Wednesday night worship team. The church also had camp meetings every year and we received from many "famous" men and women of God that were very gifted.

There was a schism forming in the church between allegiance to the Worship Pastor and the Senior Pastor. Also, there was a great deal of emphasis on scriptures about prosperity coming back to you when you give. The Word of Faith movement has a lot of great truths, including the reality that the Bible is full of promises that we can stand on, and the truth that God does want us to walk in the blessing of Abraham and prosper in all things. However, there can easily be too much emphasis placed on material blessings, and that is what we felt was happening here. I had long been influenced by George Mueller, a great man of faith who lived during the 1800's. He never accepted a salary, and only depended on voluntary offerings. He started many orphanages and always relied on God to provide everything by his simple prayers of faith, and God did!

Kerry and I both were feeling the church had gotten a little too far out on the prosperity teaching end of things, and we were struggling with attending. We really loved the worship, and much of the teaching. The church was able to bring in some great leaders in the faith – nationally and internationally known - as guest speakers, and we were learning a lot, but we were really struggling over the emphasis on prosperity. The Worship Pastor got called to start a church in another country, and many left the church, including us. We were heartbroken that the Worship Pastor was leaving; he was the one we felt most attuned with spiritually. I was in the choir and on the Wednesday night worship team, and Kerry was an usher. It was a hard decision and very painful for us.

We began attending a small church at the invitation of the worship pastor's assistant and friend. This church was also prosperity oriented, and one Sunday the Pastor said that this church was only going to be known for three things — prayer, praise and prosperity — and that evangelism and witnessing were not their calling. Now, I am not an evangelist either, but I knew that a church needed to have some kind of outreach to be balanced.

In 2000, I began working at North County Transit District (NCTD) and started a weekly Bible Study/Prayer Group during lunch, which I continued for eight years. I had been reading about how a revival in New York began with one man starting a prayer group during lunchtime and my heart was stirred. We had a very diverse group of ladies — different nationalities and different church backgrounds. Some were Catholic, some non-denominational, one a mixture of new age thinking and Christianity. My stated goal was that we learn from the Bible and allow Holy Spirit to lead into Truth, without getting sidetracked by non-Biblical doctrines or traditions. They were hungry for the Word of God and I began seeing growth in their lives.

I would often go for walks at lunch, as my office was very close to the beach. One day a homeless man was walking by as I sat on a bench, enjoying the view. He walked past then turned around suddenly, eyes blazing as they fixed upon me. He asked me, "Are you a born-again Christian?" I said, "Yes." He then began to ask me pointed questions specifically about how the church I attended would receive someone like him. He told me that he was not homeless, but actually had taken some time to walk — to Julian and back (a mountain town 60 miles away) — taking nothing with him, but relying completely upon the Lord to provide for his needs. He talked with me about covetousness, quoting the verse, "Godliness with contentment is great gain."

When he left, I was shaken to the core. I went back to my office, shut the door, got prostrate before the Lord on the floor and wept. I called Kerry and told him what had happened, saying that we could no longer attend that church. I knew God had spoken to me through that man! This verse, and the section of scriptures surrounding it, would come back to my remembrance time and time again in the years to come.

> *"If any man teach otherwise, and consent not to wholesome words, even the words of our Lord Jesus Christ, and to the*

doctrine which is according to godliness; He is proud, knowing nothing, but doting about questions and strife's of words, whereof cometh envy, strife, railings, evil surmisings, Perverse disputings of men of corrupt minds, and destitute of the truth, supposing that gain is godliness: from such withdraw thyself. But godliness with contentment is great gain. For we brought nothing into this world, and it is certain we can carry nothing out. And having food and raiment let us be therewith content. But they that will be rich fall into temptation and a snare, and into many foolish and hurtful lusts, which drown men in destruction and perdition. For the love of money is the root of all evil: which while some coveted after, they have erred from the faith, and pierced themselves through with many sorrows." I Timothy 6:3-10 (KJV)

Training

Kerry and I began going to an Apostolic/Prophetic five-fold ministry equipping church (Ephesians 4:11). I knew the minute we walked in, that this was where I belonged. The music was intense, spirit led, and Word-infused, full of prophetic declarations and apostolic thrust. I was enthralled. A woman came up to me later in the service and whispered, "I saw you in the Spirit when you came in." I wept, knowing that I was known.

Kerry agreed that this was the right church for us. We became very involved, immediately jumping in and embracing all. They had many ministry and hands-on training opportunities, meeting the needs of all and equipping for growth in Christian experience and gifts. They also had a Bible College, and I was desiring strongly to attend, but afraid. Kerry didn't want to get that involved yet, and I was afraid I would grow faster than he and didn't know how it would impact our marriage. I met with some of the leaders, and was told that as I moved forward in the spirit, Kerry's spirit would also be drawn and pulled in. I took the plunge.

It was here that I learned about Spiritual Warfare. This was a full immersion into the things of the spirit, teachings, and applications of Biblical truths that the early church walked in. The Senior Pastor was an apostolic leader with great revelation from the Word of God. It made me hungrier for the Word than I had ever been. Here I learned of the great reformers and the revivals throughout history. It was enlightening and stirring. I was inspired by the great men and women of God throughout history and what they had done to further the Kingdom. I was especially moved by John Wesley, his Holy Spirit experience with the Moravians, and all that he had accomplished in his life. I felt it was part of my history as I was raised Methodist, and saddened that the Methodist church had grown so far from its roots.

At this college we had hands-on training in prayer, prophecy, deliverance, healing, and preaching, as well as diving deep into the Word. I learned much about apostolic government, the function of the Body of Christ and how the spiritual gifts operate one with another, especially the five-fold ministry. It was here that my revelatory gifts began to grow, although it was many years before I became comfortable in the expression of them in the Body.

I served in many areas throughout our years at this church. I was part of the "Bulletin Insert" team (taking copious notes during the sermon, then typing them up and creating "bullet points" for the synopsis to be included in the following week's bulletin). As I typed the sermons, the truths revealed got into me in a greater degree than just sitting in a seat and attending. I was also on the "Publications" team and had the opportunity to write articles for the quarterly newsletter as well as assisting in the preparation of the books the Pastor was writing.

I was so hungry! The worship and prophetic environment increased the level of visions and dreams I received. I started to see that the prophetic gift within me needed to be in an atmosphere of other prophetic/apostolic people to grow. I felt I was now in a place I'd been looking for all my life, and in a company of like-minded people. The warring aspect of my spiritual DNA was being activated, and it was a huge time of growth.

I graduated with a BA in Biblical Studies. In fact, I was class Valedictorian with a 4.0 GPA! I had to give a speech to the graduating class. I hated and feared public speaking. I prepared for weeks, and went from 8 pages, single spaced, double-sided typed pages of notes, to 20 minutes of what I knew God gave me to speak. The message included a poem which, in all honesty, was one of the very best poems I have ever written. It is something that I believe every Christian can probably relate to. I was blessed to have both my daughters attend my ceremony; they were so proud of me.

During this process of intense spirit-filled immersion and instruction, my spirit (the part of us that communicates with God) became bigger than my soul (mind, will, emotions). The voices bringing condemnation, shame and guilt, were now mere whispers. The voice of Truth, heard through my spirit, shut them all down. The memories hadn't been erased from my mind, but I had more spiritual truth in me now that took authority whenever a lie came up.

While attending this church, a few other very significant things happened. They hosted a number of nationally and internationally-known, anointed, powerful ministers of the Word to come and speak. We received much laying on of hands and prophetic impartation. One of the men in particular was not only an incredibly learned man of doctrine, the level of revelation and anointing he carried was astonishing. We received a prophetic word from him that we would be successful in ministry, then he turned around and added, "and successful in business."

There was one very significant and key time of heightened spiritual awareness and activity for a two-week period at the Church, where the pastor said he wanted to provide an opportunity for those who sought and received a "word" from the Lord to share what they heard or saw. I sought the Lord and went into a vision. In the vision, I was standing on the sea and it was dark and roiling, inky blue-black, filled with souls — thousands of people drowning, the sea was full of them, calling out for help and grabbing me, screaming, "Help me; help me!" I cried out to the Lord, "Lord, what can I do?" I came out of the vision and heard, John 20:21, "*Then said Jesus to them again, Peace be unto you: as my Father hath sent me, even so I you.*" The next few verses give context. "*And when he had said this, he breathed on them, and saith unto them, Receive ye the Holy Ghost: Whosoever sins ye remit, they are remitted unto them; and whose so ever sins ye retain, they are retained.*"

This was powerful! I saw Him in the vision, and He said this to me! I was shocked and didn't really know what to do with it.

He also spoke to me, "See then that ye walk circumspectly, not as fools, but as wise, Redeeming the time, because the days are evil. Wherefore be ye not unwise, but understanding what the will of the Lord is." Ephesians 5:15 (KJV)

That Sunday I went up, in trembling and fear, and shared these! Another woman, the one behind me in line, shared that the Lord showed her the same vision, but another verse with it!

Another significant thing that occurred was regarding one of the Rhema words I had received years ago (A man's gift makes room for him and brings him before great men). I believed the gift was writing poetry. I had tried to get my spiritual poems published, and sent them to many, many publishers, and was rejected by all. Some said they were good, but they weren't accepting poetry at that time. At the same time, I experienced what I felt was rejection by some of the leaders in the church (my pride was being laid low by God, unbeknownst to me at the time), and even by Kerry who at the time told me he didn't really like my poems. (Kerry doesn't remember saying it, and says that he was not in a place where he could hear them. Now he says he can, and they are excellent.)

Regardless, what happened to me in that place left me feeling a deep hurt and rejection of my innermost being. I had not written poems since high school, and these poems were pouring out from a deep place within me. The first poem I ever wrote was during a Creative Writing class exercise in high school. During the process, something poured out of me into a beautiful poem of depths which I didn't know existed! Those early poems were not of the Holy Spirit, but they allowed something within me to be released. I had stopped writing those many years before; in fact, they got lost somewhere along the way. These new poems were more precious than gold to me, because they were from my born-again spirit released in love for the wondrous revelations I was receiving from the Father.

I cried out to the Lord during this time, because I knew Kerry was my husband and that was God's plan. Jesus became my everything, the friend that sticks closer than a brother (Proverbs 18:24) and God showed me the pride in my heart in the process.

> *"Do ye think that the scripture saith in vain, The spirit that dwelleth in us lusteth to envy? But he giveth more grace. Wherefore he saith, God resisteth the proud, but giveth grace unto the humble."*   James 4:5-6 (KJV)

Godly Lineage in Redemption

At this point in our lives, both daughters had graduated college. Sara was in a relationship with a man who loved her dearly, and had been trying to "get her" since she was 13. (She was not allowed to date at that age.) He was actually a classmate and friend of Cara's, although she ran him off from our house with a butcher knife when he came around Sara at such a young age. Cara was very protective of Sara. Once they did begin dating, I learned that he was Catholic and had some knowledge of the Bible; we had many debates that sent me searching out the Word because I knew "what" I was saying, but not "where" it came from.

They eventually did get together and were married. He won me over because he loved God and felt extremely blessed to have Sara as his wife. He truly felt she was a "catch." As a mom, I was thrilled that Sara had a man who loved her so much. Their wedding was the most beautiful I had ever experienced, and Sara designed and coordinated it all herself. It was a winter wonderland and a wonderful time of enjoyment. Many of my Maryland family were able to attend. They have two beautiful children – Cali and Keith – who are three years apart in age.

Cara also went through a very difficult and dark time during which I had to put to use the spiritual warfare weapons I had learned about. Hers is not my story to tell. It was a time in which I was very afraid as I recognized what was happening and felt powerless.

Naomi, our first grandchild, was born on Easter Sunday in 2005. When I was sharing with one of the prayer warriors at church, she prophesied that Naomi would be a deliverer. Little did I know that the first deliverance would be her mother! When Naomi was one month old, God told me to pray and fast. I did, for five days. During that time there was an intense battling in the spirit for both Cara and Naomi. Sara went to Cara and told her that she had to get out – right now - and go to our house. Cara told me years later, after she found out I had been fasting and praying, that it was as if Sara swooped in like an angel and at that moment Cara was given just enough strength to leave. Follow God's leading; your prayers matter!

They came to our house and lived with us for 18 months. It was a wonderful time of bonding with Naomi and having my relationship with Cara strengthened. We were living in Oceanside at the time, having sold our Fallbrook house to move closer to our jobs (both in Oceanside) and the girls. It was a big two-story house with a huge guest room so it was perfect for our needs. I felt such a burden for Naomi, and blessed that Kerry and I were able to be there for her and provide the stability that I had learned children need during those formative years.

Cara has since met and married a wonderful, godly man who loves her with all his heart, Naomi as his own, in fact, legally adopted her and now they have two more daughters – Zoe and Liberty! Cara and her husband both are well aware that God brought them together and are thankful for His providence, as are we!

God has truly redeemed my life and blessed me with a close relationship with my daughters, with son-in-laws who love the Lord, and with five beautiful grandchildren – four girls and one boy. My grandchildren are such a delight to my heart, as well as to Kerry. So many times God has spoken through them, and seeing the gifts that He has put in them and the blessing of being able to pray for them and speak into their lives is an amazing honor and privilege! Having children and grandchildren is also a responsibility in the spirit, and I feel the burden of the Lord for them always. Spiritual warfare, discernment and speaking words of life and blessing are necessary!

> *"Know therefore that the LORD thy God, he is God, the faithful God, which keepeth covenant and mercy with them that love him and keep his commandments to a thousand generations;"* Deuteronomy 7:9 (KJV)

Doctor's Bad Report
(Which Voice will I Believe?)

One spiritual principle I have seen over and over is that when you begin advancing spiritually, the enemy will attack to try and stop your advancement. God allows this to teach us to war. Also, there is the reality that we have to protect the territory we have taken!

One day when I was holding Naomi, one of my legs went numb from the hip and I almost fell down. I sat, and it eventually went away, but it was recurring. I had been having occasional pain, because of what I thought was my left leg being shorter than my right leg, causing my hip and pelvis area to be misaligned. I went to the doctor, and he thought it was muscular. After no improvement, I had an MRI. This was when they found out about the congenital defect of a missing nerve from the back of my left knee into my foot. However, that didn't seem to be the cause of this leg numbing problem. It seemed I had a syrnx (type of cyst) in my spinal cord. The doctor said that it could only be treated with surgery. However, because the cyst was IN the spine, it would be very dangerous to remove and probably result in paralysis from the waist down. If they did not operate, eventually it would grow and I would be paralyzed from the waist down.

So, let's see, with or without surgery, the doctor said I'd eventually be paralyzed from the waist down. This was a bad report. After the initial shock, I started toying with the idea that maybe that wouldn't be too bad. My job had become very stressful; I could go out on disability! I played with this for a few days, then my spirit kicked in. Hold on, after God had delivered me and healed me of multiple things, after I'd seen Him heal others, I was going to just stay under this negative report? No!

I began calling and emailing everyone I knew for prayer, got on every prayer line, went to healing services, studied the Word of God and wrote down in a notebook all the healing scriptures I could find and spoke them over myself daily! This went on for a long period, with no change. One day in church, I was fully worshipping, and I felt something shift. Now, mind you, it wasn't the first time I'd been fully worshipping. I am a worshipper by nature; and I love to worship. In fact, after I got over my shame of being a dancer, and saw how the devil had twisted my worshipping nature into worship of the creature versus the Creator, I vowed that as fully as I gave myself over to dance in the flesh, I would give myself even more to worshipping the One worthy of all praise and glory and honor! So, this wasn't the first time I'd fully been worshipping, but something happened. I went back to the doctor, got another MRI, and there was no indication of the cyst in my spine. All praise to the Glory of God!

Shortly thereafter, I was able to share my testimonies of healing that I and others had experienced, to our neighbor who had had multiple treatments for lung cancer. He gladly let me pray for him, and I found out three years later that he had not had any more recurrences!

Our testimonies hold the same power that brought deliverance and healing for us; when we share them; others are empowered to lay hold with faith and receive!

I am the Lord that Healeth Thee

I am the Lord that healeth thee
Open your eyes and you will see;
I am the author
Of Eternity.

You were created in glory
And to glory will be
Is there anything too hard for Me?
Look to Me always, look to Me!

Holy Spirit Discernment

The wonderful church we were attending began to experience rifts. The enemy was on the move to destroy the church and its influence in the region. I am not going to go into great detail about the things that happened. It was heartbreaking for all involved.

There were many times that Kerry and I felt and heard the Spirit of God, but we didn't have enough confidence to speak out. We were intimidated by the "greater" callings upon some of the leaders, and felt they must be right and we must be wrong. In fact, Holy Spirit told me specifically one thing that had happened before it became "news" and I thought it was my own evil, suspicious mind!

The last straw for us is that we had a guest speaker come to the church, a preacher who had been miraculously delivered from prison, and the calling on his life was very strong. He brought a strong word that included an area needing correction in the church. I was leading a team that developed the bulletin inserts at the time, and it was my week to summarize the points from the sermon. I was so thankful that someone brought up this issue. I believed it was needed for the whole body to walk in greater purity. I was told by staff that it had to be removed.

I fought back, stating strongly that it was the most important point and something that had to be incorporated, but was shut down. Kerry completely agreed. I ended up sending a long letter to the Pastor and leaders, explaining that we could no longer attend. I never heard from the Pastor; I don't even know if he ever even knew about it. The response I did get came from one of the leaders under him. The bottom line is that they didn't include the point that I knew God was wanting to address in the church, so we left.

It wasn't until a few years later that we both recognized that we actually *were* hearing from Holy Spirit each of the times that we thought we were hearing, but must be wrong because other, *"greater"* men and women of God were not hearing what we were. It was many years later that we heard someone speak of the necessity of every member of the Body of Christ participating and sharing what they hear, for the "full counsel" of God, according to I Corinthians 12:7 (KJV) *"But the manifestation of the Spirit is given to every man to profit withal."*

We had invested our heart and soul, years of time and many funds into this church. It was heartbreakingly painful to leave, and difficult. Most of the people we were close to had already left, but there were still many attending that we loved dearly.

The Holy Spirit led us to a wonderful, Spirit-filled church in the area full of very committed and humble servants of the Lord. We immediately got involved in prayer ministry – intercessory ministry before the service, the altar ministry after services. I also attended the mid-week, early morning, prayer teams. Eventually we started leading a home group. We were with this wonderful group of men and women for a few years and are blessed to still minister with some of them in other capacities throughout the region.

Godly Favor Brings Advancement

At work, a position had become open for a Management Analyst. I had absolutely no desire to apply for that position, as it called for experience in statistics! A spirit-filled friend told me that she thought the position was for me. I discounted it; I didn't even fully meet the qualifications! No one was hired and it was reposted. The third time it was posted, she said strongly, "Alane, I know that Holy Spirit is telling me that this is your job." I agreed to apply, although I still had no desire for the position, because she insisted Holy Spirit told her that it was for me.

I was the only one who passed the test, through all three postings! I had prayed that if this was God's will I would get the job. I wanted to be faithful to His leading, and trusted Him. The Director told me that she felt "led" to give me the job. She knew my work habits, and quality of work, as I was under one of her managers already as the Document Control Administrator, so I had "proven" my faithfulness with what I was given to that point.

As I met with her, she explained that Management Analyst was a very fluid position, depending on the department needs. What they needed was an "Americans with Disabilities Act (ADA)" expert, so that was my primary task — to become an expert in that arena! I had other duties - typing up and/or editing Board reports for all the Managers, filing, doing research, etc., but this "project" became my baby and it soon became apparent that God was in the middle of it.

This was a time of great favor. I sunk my teeth into this project; I loved research, as well as rules and regulations. All of my jobs with government (State of Maryland, County of Lehigh in Pennsylvania, City of San Diego) had included interpretation of ordinances, rules, and regulations of some kind. I had no knowledge of ADA up to this point, but was keenly aware of Civil Rights Issues. I was in fourth grade when desegregation occurred, living in Maryland where there was a strong Ku Klux Klan. I had always been a champion of the underdog, so this seemed a perfect fit for me.

I did some searching online about the ADA, and as "luck" would have it (haha, totally God's timing; I don't believe in "luck"), the very next month the National Association of ADA Coordinators was holding their semi-annual conference, and it was in San Diego! I got approval to attend.

Attending the conference was like being immersed in a foreign language. Oh my, so many Federal regulations that agencies and local governments must comply with. One of the things I learned, upon hearing the regulations and then going back to NCTD and doing some historical research, was that NCTD was not in compliance with some very basic fundamentals, especially in the area of administrative requirements. They, like many transit agencies, thought that if they were in compliance with the service regulations, the administrative regulations didn't apply.

It was very difficult, being the new kid on the block and trying to tell career transit managers and directors that they were out of compliance. I formed a team, representatives from each department, bringing them up to speed with the requirements. Some were resistant, most accepting and willing to do the work of self-evaluation of policies, programs, facilities and services. However, this was going to be a very long process and involve a tremendous amount of time and effort, and those over them weren't very supportive.

However, God had His plans. Shortly after this initial meeting, we received a Federal complaint from one of our riders, and it was an over-arching complaint that involved many departments. As part of the Federal investigation, we were required by them to do an agency-wide compliance review and it had a short deadline! So, we had to hire a firm with which I would oversee. Serendipitous? You tell me!

The end result was that, over the course of months, we did a lot of work and created a plan which was then incorporated into budget years, with timelines for completion. There was a lot of resistance to the status quo and my message was not well received. One of the things that occurred during all of this is that the Director who hired me to be Management Analyst became Executive Director. She was very pro-ADA, and this helped my "cause" immensely. During her time as Executive Director, I was able to implement many grant funded programs that provided increased service and efficiency, as well as reducing our overall costs. It was a wonderful time of growth and expansion for the District and myself.

In fact, during this time God led me to start a Non-Profit and divinely orchestrated my meeting the people that would be part of the development. I had favor with NCTD to do this while working there, and to allot some of my time towards this until we received grant funding, hired staff and became self-sufficient. We named it Full Access and Coordinated Transportation (FACT). This all came about because I was getting calls from people that needed service (elderly and/or people with disabilities) but did not qualify for paratransit, or were outside the service area. It broke my heart and sent me to prayer.

I began searching to find out what was available for them. This led me to search what other agencies were doing. It couldn't possibly be that NCTD was the only agency with this problem, and I found out about coordination. Easter Seals Project Action was providing a "Mobility Services Planning Institute" and picked twenty teams from the U.S. to allow to attend through an application process. I went to multiple meetings, and agencies, private and public, trying to get someone to spearhead this worthwhile project, and, although everyone thought it was a great idea, no one wanted to take the lead. So, by default, I took the lead, because I knew it had to be done.

The idea was to coordinate resources from existing transportation agencies, public and private, to meet some of the needs. FACT is still in existence today, although the name changed somewhat and it is really a brokerage rather than true coordination as envisioned originally. This was the most exciting and rewarding project I had ever undertaken, to that point. It was creating something from nothing, starting with a vision, letting God lead the way and bring the right people together in His timing. It was truly birthed from prayer.

Over the course of my ten years at NCTD, I received four promotions. One of them, I think the third, God had told me to the penny in a dream exactly what the increase would be. And it was, ...two years later! The first year, I did get a raise, but it wasn't what God had told me and I was very angry, feeling the devil was impeding the will of God. In fact, my pride and impatience was. God was teaching me about His timing and about remaining humble and trusting Him. I didn't do very well during that testing period, although eventually I did get the point, and the raise, to the exact penny!

My life at this time seemed to be a continuum of advancement and favor. My salary had nearly doubled from when I started at NCTD, I was managing numerous grants and staff. The paratransit budget alone was over $4,000,000! I had to learn a lot about planning and budgeting, justification and reporting. I had become an expert in the ADA and was speaking in public about our programs at State and Federal conferences. I truly loved my job and was amazed at how my life had changed. Things were going really well. Time to be on guard! (Hindsight is 20/20, they say.)

Shocked by a Dream

While at NCTD, during this time of great advancement and favor, God was also moving in my life in another realm. On January 5, 2007, I woke up from a very strange dream, with a blinding migraine headache. I had been fasting for a few days, but not by choice (I had had the stomach flu). It is very interesting to me that many times when I had sensed God calling me to fast, and I didn't obey, I would "mysteriously" get some kind of a stomach virus that forced me to fast!

In the dream, I was in a large auditorium that was filled with all the people in my life who had impacted my spiritual journey. I began talking to a woman who, in the natural, was a young mom, married only a year or so, and who worked full-time. In the dream, she told me that she had written a book. I was surprised, and asked her the title. "Moses — Shocked in the Desert," she responded. "Wow," I said, "That's awesome." Then I thought about it for a minute or two and said, "Wait a minute, how do you have time to write? I know I have been called to write, and I don't have time to." Then I woke up.

I lay there, knowing that it was clearly a God dream, and asking what it meant. Part of me just wanted to go back to sleep, but I knew this was from God. After some more questioning of God, I felt that God was telling me to write a book with that title. I asked, and received that confirmation from the witness of the Holy Spirit. So, I got up and went into the other room to write down the title, knowing that if didn't do that, there would be a good chance I would not remember the title in the morning.

I went back to bed. I lay there, unable to sleep, still with a migraine, and then "heard" the impression of some scriptures about Moses and the journey to the Promised Land. Now I knew that I definitely would not remember those, so I went and wrote those down also, along with other things the Holy Spirit was revealing about the scriptures He led me to. Then I did go back to bed, for a brief time before having to get up and go to work.

The next night, 2:00 in the morning, another awakening with a migraine. There was no dream this time, but I was feeling the impression of scriptures. I got up and wrote what I heard, then got ready for work.

The third night, the same thing happened, so I said to God, "Okay, I get it, you want me to write this book. How about no more headaches, and I will agree to get up and write when you wake me." I also told God that if this was really Him, that I was willing, but that the whole thing, all the way through the process, had to be fully Him. In other words, I was not going to try and make things happen in my own way (been there, done that, doesn't work) and He would have to bring the right people at the right time, show me the way, open the doors, etc. I had learned that lesson with the poems, and with FACT!

So, the process of most of the writing of the book took place over about 12-18 months, with me waking between 2-3 a.m., writing, then, going to work at my full-time, high responsibility job! I had complete grace for it and continued to prosper at work during this time. Whenever I had doubts (often), I'd ask God if it was really Him, did He really tell me to write a book, and He would whisper in my spirit another scripture or revelation about certain sections of the book.

After the bulk of the writing was finished, then came the process of typing the notes. Yes, these were all written as journal entries, so they had to be typed up. I took a week of my vacation time the next year to do that. What a mess! As I was typing, I was thinking, "Oh my gosh, how in the world am I going to be able to put this into some kind of order?"

That was the next step, and it required a great deal of prayer and pressing in to the Lord, because it didn't make any sense to me as to how I could organize the book. I had received many different revelations, at different times, on one scripture! So, do I put the book in chronological order by book of the Bible? But that wouldn't work because many of the scriptures He gave me to "back up" a point He made came from many other areas of scripture. I stopped trying to figure it out and waited until I got inspiration.

Eventually, Holy Spirit showed me that it was to be written by "topic" and gave me the "shocking" section headings to use. I loved the idea, because that's how I like to read non-fiction books – find a section in the Table of Contents that appeals to me at the moment (led by Holy Spirit), then read that!

After each main task, I'd have to set the book aside for a while. I tend to put

150% of my energy into things, then get sick of it because I've pushed myself too hard in excitement and zeal.

So, again, everything was going pretty good...

Sometime during the process of writing the book, after having been with our new church for a few years, Kerry was feeling that he needed "more" of the Spirit. I didn't disagree, although I really enjoyed the family we'd grown into at our church. Our home group had changed as people moved and new people came in. Some friends of ours joined our group, although they actually didn't go to our church, and the man wanted us to try out using some CDs of teaching that he was really enjoying. We checked one out, and it was okay, and we probably should not have gone along with it, but it was at a time when it was "easier" than having to prepare every week. Well, then it became a problem. We felt the teachings were a little off doctrinally, but we didn't want to hurt the man's feelings.

At the same time, we heard about another church where there was more movement of the Spirit during services. Now that we had recovered from the pain experienced with the breakup of the apostolic/prophetic church where we had been very involved, we realized that there was still validity and truth — a spiritual reality — with depths that we weren't walking in at our current church. We really longed for the voice of the prophetic.

At this new church, we saw some of the people who had left the other church, and met many others who were "prophetically" inclined. I had learned, as had Kerry, that we had to be around prophetic people to have our own prophetic gifts activated. One of the most impactful books I read during Bible College was "Apostolic Strategies Affecting Nations" by Dr. Jonathan David. It contains very detailed information about the five-fold gifts of Apostle, Prophet, Teacher, Pastor and Evangelist and how they interact with each other. One of the things I had read that really rang true was that if you are a prophet (or prophetically inclined), in order to grow in your calling you will need to be able to receive from an Apostle or Prophet. I have found this to be true.

The Senior Pastor was very gifted in discernment of people's gifts and loved helping people grow into their callings. There were many times that he (and others) prophesied over us. In fact, here I received two prophetic words about being an author, and no one there knew I was writing a book! Kerry and I were moved to bring a word at times, and were also asked to preach one Sunday. We met some incredibly gifted spiritual leaders here who had their own ministries, some of whom have become life-long partners and friends.

"That Can't Be God!"

In 2008, we had a change in management at my work. My job went from being a dream job to being a nightmare. There were many cuts being made to reduce costs across the board, and this translated to many managers being rearranged, reassigned and redirected, as well as eliminated for restructure of the organization. I was under a lot of pressure; as the service parameters changed, so did the paratransit service boundaries, bringing an increase in complaints. I had a new supervisor that loved to push the buttons of those under him. He was outrageously extroverted, offsetting the intense pressure of the job with humor, but his intensity created more tension.

My best friend retired, as did many others I was close to. I began to hear, "You should look into retirement." I knew that God had given me this job, and brought such favor along the way, that this voice could not possibly be His!

In 2009, I was asked to take on another department – Customer Service. It was couched in terms of "We really like what you did to improve the Paratransit service; we would like you to do the same with Customer Service." The layoffs and doubling of duties in other areas was noted, along with the desire of management to keep me as an employee. I didn't have to be a rocket scientist to read between those lines. There was a minimal increase in pay and an increase of one-week vacation, but a warning that there would be no increase in personnel to assist in the duties.

This was a challenging time. My husband and I were struggling emotionally, and I was getting emotional needs met through friends and work. We became offended by something at church (red flag). I was too busy to lead the work Bible study anymore, as I was working through lunch every day, and we stopped ministry.

Christmas Day 2009 I ended up in the hospital emergency room. I had not been feeling well for a few days and it was getting progressively worse. The usual home treatments weren't helping. After our family gathering, I thought maybe a hot bath would help. At that point, I noticed my abdomen was red and swollen; I looked five months pregnant! Alarmed, I got out and called

Kaiser. After many questions, I was told to go to the nearest emergency room immediately (non-Kaiser). By the time I was seen by the attending physician, I was throwing up bile and my temperature was nearly 105! An ultrasound revealed that a gallstone was stuck in the neck of the gallbladder. My gallbladder was completely infected and the infection had spread to the liver. Two shots of morphine did not help with the pain; they had to put me on medical grade Heroin.

I was transported by ambulance to Kaiser Hospital. For five days, I could not even suck on ice chips without throwing up. I was told later that if I hadn't gone to the hospital when I did, I would have become septic and might have died. After seven days, I was released with oral antibiotics and other drugs.

I had to wait 30 days to have my gallbladder removed, to ensure the infection was completely out of my system. While I was recuperating at home, I heard the Lord say to me, "I have picked you up and plucked you out; you are done there." Oh my; it *was* the Lord telling me to look into retirement!

When I went back to work, I determined (based on my age, and other factors) that I would "officially" retire at the end of June, 2010. The next six months were very challenging. Even though I knew the Lord was telling me to quit, and that I'd almost died, I still loved most of my job. I also loved the money, my projects, the trips to conferences I got to take, the "Name" I now had as an ADA expert (speaking at conferences, the spokesperson for NCTD on ADA, etc.). Doubts were creeping in, along with general reluctance and bargaining with God. He won, of course. I was actually shocked at the reluctance I had to quitting, especially the pull of fame and fortune! I really didn't know that was in me. I used to be a hippie, for Pete's sake, and at one time didn't care at all about material things.

The reality of what had happened to me, the need to finish the book, and my strong desire in the spirit to live for God, along with the desire to be closer physically to the kids and grandkids, eventually won the internal fight. As difficult as it was, I knew that it was the right time.

We put our big two-story house on the market and it sold in three days, at the top end of our range! We bought a mobile home in San Diego close to the kids, so I could retire and finish the book, do whatever God would lead me to, and spend more time with the kids and grandkids. Sara's first baby, a girl, had been born in 2008, so now I had double blessings to enjoy! The first day Sara came to our new home, she wept with gratitude, noting how long it had been since we'd lived close to her.

Calling Forth into New Identity

The year 2010 was pivotal in so many ways. I turned 55, we retired and we downsized greatly. Our lifestyle changed as we went from having plenty of money to do what we wanted to do, to having to be very careful with our money. We were not sure how it was all going to work out in the long run, but we were determined to trust God and obey.

That summer, Cara married a wonderful, Godly man who loved Naomi as his own, and they had a "destination" wedding in Mexico. It was so beautiful, and the two granddaughters were flower girls! A big surprise to us was that they asked Kerry to perform the service! What a blessing! I believe this was also a significant stepping forward into the calling upon our marriage. It should have been no surprise that a great battle had taken place in the year prior, one in which the prophetic calling and destiny of our marriage had been at a pivotal point.

In fact, when the Holy Spirit reminded me of the vision God gave me for our marriage on Christmas night, 1993, and showed me in the spirit what would happen to my destiny, Kerry's destiny, and the destinies of our children and grandchildren, it was not even a choice anymore. I saw the gravity of choices, as well as the subtle, seducing deception of the enemy and it roused up the warrior in me to combat the enemy as never before. The prophetic promises over my life have to be brought back to my remembrance often, to encourage me as challenges come in the area of God's formation of a new identity.

A very important piece of the new identity was, of course, coming into the identity of author and "owning" this new identity. This was not an easy process for me. It has taken years of breaking down insecurity, fear, performance addiction, my habit of trying to "hurry up and get to the next thing on my list," which does not really work when you are writing.

The next step in this was to try and edit the book myself. God hadn't led me to any editors. Much of my career had included editing other people's reports and English had been my best subject in school. Also, I had a little experience with publications from the Apostolic/Prophetic church we had been involved in. As I was editing the book, when I got to the part about King Asa (the chapter entitled "SHOCKING: God honors vows made with our lips, even when we have forgotten them.") Holy Spirit reminded me of the "It's time" word I had received from God years before. ("If you don't live for me, you're out of here.")

I was SHOCKED. How could I have forgotten that incredible, life-changing Rhema word, confirmed with Cara calling about her nightmare the next morning? I was so thankful and humbled that God chose to spare my life! He also reminded me as I was editing the chapter entitled "What You Mutter Matters" that I had been saying multiple times daily, over the last year or so, "This stress is killing me." Wow...this book was not just something to write and publish, but God was using it to speak to me and reveal things that I hadn't seen of His ways in my own life!

Transition
(Out of the Old and Into the New)

Since I retired in 2010, it seems my life is in continual transition. It wasn't just becoming used to being thought of and known as an "author." It really has been the transition from the world's mindset to Kingdom mindset. I had not fully realized just how deeply the world system of thinking is embedded within. It isn't just living a godly, moral life when you are born again. To truly be a new creature, our minds have to be transformed. The real transformation is from being our own god to letting God be God, and trusting Him for everything.

This was easier when I was first born again; I was a single mom and didn't have much money, I didn't really have any friends as my lifestyle had changed radically. It was easy to immerse myself in church and I was truly dependent on God. Over the years that changed; as my work situation became more secure, I learned about retirement and 401K's. Planning for the future became important, as I wanted to have something to leave my kids when I died. My father was very good with money and investments and we talked about it often. Over time, my thoughts about money became more and more conformed to the world's way of thinking. After I "became" the ADA expert at NCTD, my identity subtly shifted. I've already talked about these things in previous chapters. Yet there is an important piece I need to address at greater measure, as it keeps reappearing and the Holy Spirit has been revealing more depth to Kingdom mindset.

It's one thing to read, *"Seek ye first the Kingdom of God and His righteousness and all these things will be added unto you."* Matthew 6:3 (KJV). That verse is used a lot to keep us focused on our priorities and trusting God. However, Jesus also said that it is easier for a camel to go through the eye of a needle than a rich man to enter the Kingdom of God (Mark 10:25). Wow! Why is that? I can tell you that the world system is one whose god is Mammon — money. That is how it operates. Also, the love of pleasure and being our own god is the focus. In the Old Testament, the journey of the Israelites to the Promised Land is one of God leading them through the wilderness to teach them that *"Man does not live by bread only but by every word that proceeds from the mouth of the Lord."* (Deuteronomy 8:3; Matt. 4:4). They had been slaves for so long that they were used to following orders and having their needs met, but God wanted to build relationship with them and teach them moment by moment to trust Him. It is still that way in Kingdom mindset.

For me, this is a continual process because we are *in* the world but not *of* it. The washing of the feet symbolizes that well. We are clean when born again, but where we walk in our daily life brings "dirt" onto us, or "worldly thinking." I get up in the morning and spend time with the Lord in prayer and the Word, then go out where the focus of talk is money, fear and pleasure. Or I go on Facebook, read the paper, watch TV, listen to the radio, talk to family or friends, and wherever their mind is, whatever their "god" is, influences the conversation. So God has been transitioning me, re-aligning me little by little, to Kingdom mindset, trusting Him in the moment and letting Him order my days and bring His plans into my present.

The seeking first the Kingdom isn't just starting my day off right by communing with God through prayer and reading the Bible; it is always re-positioning my mind to looking to Him when situations arise, to the reality that God's provision is endless – He is sovereign and He influences others to bring what I need. This is shown throughout scripture, from Elijah being fed by the ravens and the widow of Zarephath (just one example among many), the Israelites getting water from the rock and manna from the sky, to the donkey being made ready for Jesus, the coin in the mouth of the fish that Jesus told Peter to get, etc. These aren't just fairy tales or fables, this is Kingdom.

Then there is the dimension of God using us to speak to other people – giving us the words to say, providing healing in the name of Jesus, etc. These are all Kingdom paradigms versus us having superficial conversations or going into agreement with what the world, the devil and our/their flesh says about a situation. Kingdom...we align to the Divine.

Identity Thief

The timing of an attempt to steal my identity in the natural is so apparent, in hindsight. God was trying to show me something! The thief comes to steal, kill and destroy. One of my biggest fears had been identity theft.

Now, the true fear wasn't someone operating in my identity; it was having everything exposed and having financial security destroyed. There have been numerous instances where this fear manifested. My faith that God holds my future, and is the source of my identity, has been tested. In fact, He had been going to the very root of the fear, as I will explain later.

There is a significant connection to identity and security. Where my identity is rooted is key to how secure I feel in it. If my identity is in the world system (money, fame, looks), my security is transitory. If my identity is truly in Christ, who is eternal and the source of all things - by Him was everything made that was made (John 1:3, Colossians 1:13), then I am secure in all areas. God was taking me through a process of letting go of every aspect of identity not rooted in His Eternal purposes!

STOLEN PURSE

A few years after I retired, I went to the beach with my youngest daughter and her two children. I was in a mental state where I was very scattered and distracted. When we got to the parking lot (which was in a very "sketchy" area and many transients frequented), I put my purse on the floor in the back and covered it up with a blanket. I took my phone and my car keys with me, made sure the windows were up and locked the door.

When I returned to my car, I saw a big dark spot under the car. It looked like a puddle of water, and it was puzzling to me as it was a sunny day. As I got closer, it looked like one of the back windows was open. I thought, "Oh my gosh, did I leave the window open?" Yet I knew I hadn't done that. Then, as I looked closer I saw that there were little bits of glass in the rubber seal. It dawned on me at that point, that my window had been broken out. In fact, it had been cut completely out and was the source of the "puddle" under the car. The whole window was in one piece, on the pavement under the car! My next thought was, "Oh no, my purse!" Yes, it was gone. My wallet with all my credit cards, driver's license and cash (only $8.00), my MP3 player, glasses and house keys! "Oh no, not the house keys; now they have my license with the house address and the house keys too!" Fear gripped my heart.

I immediately called the police and they said they were on the way. I called Kerry and told him to call every credit card company to alert them to the theft. I approached every person in the parking lot area and asked if they had seen anything. They all said they had not. I was afraid and angry! I was praying like crazy as I looked around the area, in the trash cans, etc. Then I got angrier and said, "Oh no you don't, devil. I am praying and declaring that whatever was stolen is going to be restored to me 100 times, and that whoever listens to my MP3 player full of Christian songs will be saved!"

The police came and took the report, telling me it was very common there and they would be looking for the purse. I didn't have much hope of them finding it, to be honest. I drove home in a panic, hoping and praying the thieves wouldn't be there and hadn't already been there and robbed us. I thought about all that I would have to do – change the locks, get a new license, and replace all the credit cards, bank card; what a nightmare!

I was halfway home when the phone rang. It was the police; they had found my purse in a trash can in another nearby parking lot! The money in my wallet was gone, as were a few credit cards, but not my license or house keys. I called Kerry right away; he hadn't even been able to contact all of the companies yet! I was so relieved at the end result, and exuberantly thanked the police for their effort and success!

A few weeks later I received a consulting job that resulted in getting paid $8,000! Remember, I lost $8.00 and declared 100-fold return? This was a 1,000-fold return! Praise God!

COMPUTER SCAMMERS

A few years after the purse was stolen, I had a bad experience with computer scammers. I try to be very careful on the computer. One of my sons-in-law is very knowledgeable in this area and I often relied on him to "fix" my computer when it was slow or unresponsive (or worse). He warned me each time about going to unsafe sites or downloading programs and opening email attachments.

One day when I was on the computer a pop-up notice appeared saying that my computer was slow and memory almost full. At that time I was not feeling well physically and was also mentally scattered, fretting and anxious. I was also obsessing about something that I was trying to make happen, using the computer for searching for the best deals (which exacerbated the fretting).

In the pop-up, there was a link to click on for "help." Now, I knew enough not to click on this link. I remembered a program I once had that would "clean up" the computer and make it more efficient. I began to search for that program and thought I found it. When I called the help number, they asked if they could have access to my computer and "see" what was going on. They offered to install a program that would help my computer run more efficiently. I agreed. I can hear you cringing as you read this.

Immediately after I allowed them access and paid for the service contract, I became very paranoid, so much so that I became convinced I had been duped and my identity was not secure. I was too embarrassed to tell my son-in-law. I called them back immediately and told them I wanted to cancel the contract. They were very aggressive in trying to change my mind, but I did prevail.

My paranoia became worse. I spent days on the computer trying to uninstall all the pieces of the programs that were installed to "help." I changed all my passwords, but was paranoid they could "see" my keystrokes. I was a mess. After a few days, my husband became very concerned as well, not about the identity issues, but about my state of mind and spirit. I could not find peace. At one point I did think to look up the antibiotic side effects and found that it should be taken with food, which the pharmacist neglected to tell me. Also, one of the potential side effects was paranoia and anxiety!

Even after some of the symptoms subsided, I was still anxious and troubled. I could not concentrate enough to even read the Word of God or pray. I was in dire straits. I was crying out for help and the Holy Spirit reminded me about a book I had read many years back, "Deliver Us from Evil," by Don Basham. I picked it up and read some of it again. I became convinced that this was a spiritual battle and told Kerry we needed to pray this off.

We began to pray that attacks and curses be broken, the enemy's tactics bound, etc. As we persisted, I got a picture of my father, then my paternal grandmother, and perceived that this was a generational spirit of anxiety that needed to be broken. So we did that, and laid the ax to the root in generations past. I have not been troubled by that intensity of anxiety since. I pray and believe it will not be manifested in subsequent generations. My youngest daughter had been prone to this spirit of anxiety in her life also, and she has not mentioned any attacks since that prayer time.

I have had recurring dreams of having my purse stolen after leaving it somewhere, and other identity theft type dreams (nightmares). In the dream, I would go back and look for it and be very upset that it was gone, or all my money and identification stolen. However, in the most recent "stolen purse" dream in 2017, there has been a shift. In that dream, when I realized I had left my purse somewhere and went to look for it, it was right where I left it and nothing was stolen! Progress; praise the Lord!

WHAT GOD IS SAYING

During and after these attacks, it became clear what the Spirit of the Lord was saying. Kerry had been telling me that I was going to have to wrestle with the Lord on this matter, as my source had to be Him alone. He was to be my security *and* my identity! This was a season of great shifting in my life, and the upheaval was causing the roots of false identity to come to the surface so that they could be purged from me.

Identity

Look to me and you will see
The source of your identity.
Your desire for security
Can only be fulfilled in Me.

And when I decree that it is so,
All things go where I say go.

You know from times past that I provide

So why in the world do you long to hide
In the system in which I do not abide?

I have told you My kingdom is not of this world,
And you have watched as things are unfurled
From the hidden to the manifest.
My plans and provision are always for your best.

So look to me and be set free
From false identity and security.
What I provide is outside of this realm
Of the systems with power and greed at the helm.

So look to me and be set free
From the things of this world you must flee
Turn to me, turn to me,
Your eyes will be opened to truly see
The riches of glory in eternity.

I will make you truly blessed
With identity and security that comes from rest;
Resting that comes from trusting my ways
For I am eternal, the ancient of days.

All things are mine and what is mine is yours
My presence brings blessing that upon you pours
Through my ways –
The opening of doors.

Throughout our journey, God had been slowly, but surely leading Kerry and me to spirit-filled ministries and groups that were moving in the gifts of the Spirit. I became aware that there were others like me out there. In 2012, we began attending a weekly gathering where the gifts flowed like honey under the apostolic leaders' facilitation of the movement of the Holy Spirit. My gifts began coming forth and I was encouraged to express what was in me.

I began to feel safe to share about the book in these settings, and found that I wasn't outcast, shamed, or mocked! These gatherings, and the people that attended, have become integral to my calling manifesting. The worship created an environment where Holy Spirit moved among us and I shared what He was showing me. Others shared what they saw and heard. It is an amazing thing to behold, seeing and hearing how the Spirit of Christ is revealed through a many membered body, and how we jointly rise higher. There is a knitting together that occurs, a bonding that reveals the heart of God and His family being joined.

In 2010, Kerry and I began attending and eventually became leaders in a very large non-denominational church. I am a leader in one of the Women's ministries, and have also had the opportunity to share my testimony at a small group, then a large campus-wide retreat to nearly 500 women. Afterwards, many women came up to me, some weeping, that they had been delivered from a lifetime of shame, from believing they were crazy, and from mental confusion as they identified with parts of my testimony! Over the next few days, many more stopped me to testify of the impact of my testimony in setting them free. In addition, I've been able to teach from "Moses – Shocked in the Desert" at this church, and most of the attendees in the class have testified that their lives were changed! Some began hearing God for the first time!

A significant measure of healing took place as I shared my testimony in public. The enemy had kept me bound in fear for years because of my testimony; fear from shame of my sins and fear of man's reaction at the power of God in my life being shared – that I was "crazy," that the things that I experienced were mental illness or illusion or imagination, fear that no one would believe me. I know now that it was the enemy keeping me bound because there is power in our testimonies. "*They overcame by the blood of the Lamb and the word of their testimony and they loved not their lives unto the death.*" Revelation 12:11 (KJV)

It was at this large non-denominational church that Kerry and I formed a ministry to meet the needs of the elderly in convalescent or assisted living facilities. We had been attending this church for many years and there had been times I wanted to venture out into a smaller church with more freedom in the flowing of the service, but we were not released to do that. Instead, we seem to have developed this type of service in the ministry that we provide to the elderly. God's ways are not our ways!

God is doing a mighty work in the region of San Diego. In August 2012, a well-known prophet came to San Diego and prophesied that San Diego would be key to bringing revival to the nation, and that it would be from a unified sound. In subsequent years there has been a unity growing among the Body of Christ here, in facilitating worship events and outreaches that bring people from many different churches. We are becoming the many membered Body in the spirit of Unity, and His spirit is flowing like oil down Aaron's beard.

> "*{A Song of degrees of David.} Behold, how good it is for brethren to dwell together in unity! It is like the precious ointment upon the head, that ran down upon the beard, even Aaron's beard: that went down to the skirts of his garments; As the dew of Hermon, and as the dew that descended upon the mountains of Zion: for there the LORD commanded the blessing, even life for evermore.*" Psalm 133:1-3 (NIV)

This is the ascent of alignment that brings Kingdom assignments! People are being set free throughout this region, free from religious mindsets, enabled to live daily in relationship with the Living God and being activated to fulfill the calling of God upon their lives!

Trusting God in the Midst of Pain

In August 2015, my mom died. Although she had had multiple physical conditions, and was 88 years old, her death was a shock. My dad had passed in 2011, and his physical condition had been deteriorating and was very noticeable in appearance. My mom, on the other hand, had been looking better than she had in years when she passed. In fact, she had come out here to visit the month before and we all had a wonderful time.

A number of things had been happening that led my Mom, in January of 2015, to go into an assisted living situation. She did not want her children to be the ones forced into making that decision and she felt the Lord leading her to take that step.

In July, my mom traveled to visit her brothers and sister, and then came to our home to visit with us for 10 days. It was a joyful time; she spent time with her "California" children, grandchildren, and great-grandchildren, meeting the 4th great-grandchild for the first time. She looked wonderful and it was a blessed time.

After she went back home, a few short weeks later she fell and ended up in the hospital. Nothing was broken, and after a few days they were going to release her. Then some aberrations in behavior led me to realize that she was not doing well at all. She was talking nonsensically, hallucinating and said she was in a lot of pain. I talked to the nurse and the nurse said my mom was not on any medication that would cause behaviors like that. The next day my mom was in a lot of pain and her mind was worse.

I called my sister Joy and told her we had to go back; "something" told me she was dying. We made the reservation for two days later. The next day, one of my sisters back there told me that she had been visiting my mom and the doctor came in and said that the diseases in her lungs, kidney, and heart were putting a great strain on her system and that the medicine to treat each had a negative effect on the other. He asked when all the family would be together, as some decisions would have to be made. My sister said our mom was glaring at the doctor when he said this.

The next morning, I got up at 4:00 a.m. to get to the airport by 5 for our flight. I checked my phone and there was a missed call and missed text from my brother. My mom had passed at 2 a.m. I yelled out, "NO, GOD!!!!" I was so angry. I could not believe that He would let this happen.

This was a difficult time. There were some long-standing issues with my youngest sister that would manifest during the next week and months, legal issues that needed to be addressed, as well as financial. It was a very hard time with many years of undelivered communications and resentments among siblings. Anger would come to the surface and be addressed and healed.

Eventually I realized that my mother died the way she lived — refusing to be a burden in any way to her children. I believe that when the doctor asked my sister when the family would be there, she decided right then and there that it was time to go, and had a little conversation with God about it. She was a very strong Christian and, ultimately, how and when a person dies is up to God and He knows the perfect time. The Holy Spirit counseled me greatly over the next six months and beyond about this. I am at peace, but I still miss her greatly. The last years I had with both my parents were filled with wonderful testimonies of God's faithfulness, sharing our mutual love for Him and each other.

I am grateful for the good qualities that I have received from both of my parents, and the strong ethical values they imparted to me. My parents were both worshipers, loved Church and good preaching of the Word of God. Both of my parents were very intelligent and valued hard work and discipline. These are traits that I have received and they have served me well.

Re-test of Key Test

In January 2015, another test came. January always seems to be a transitional time for me, a time of re-evaluation of my life and where it was going. I was jealous of others who seemed to have more freedom in the money arena. Specifically, I was jealous of those that seemed to take lots of trips, especially to Hawaii!

I was also struggling with having to "promote myself" which is how I was viewing marketing of the book. I was still struggling with the reality that "God gave me this book to write," and having to say that in public. I was coming face to face with the old "you're crazy" voice and it was time for a face-off. In the publishing industry, if you don't already have a "platform" (being a Pastor, or some other area of expertise, with followers) you need to build a platform by promotion of the book. I felt that if God wanted it bought, He would bring people to buy it. Of course, that is true, but if the author isn't letting people know about it, how can they?

Two things were at play here. I wasn't comfortable with the stretching, and my desire for money. Realistically, I knew that I had to make an effort to promote the book. I had done a few book signings, and shared about the book in my small, safe network. We were attending a large, doctrinally sound church with hundreds of ministries. I first shared about the book in the women's ministry where I had become a leader. I was astonished to find that as I shared my story, others were set free! It was a very small setting - perhaps 50 women - and they knew and trusted me. It was not that difficult for me to share about the book in that setting. It was a very different task to put it out there where "regular" Christians and non-Christians could potentially attack me for my past or mock me.

So, that was going on internally. In our finances, we were in a place where it was still challenging since I had made good money when I was working full-time, and now it was hit or miss. I was doing some temporary assignments — clerical work, proctoring tests, selling personal things on E-Bay, cutting down on unnecessary spending, etc., but perusing the "Jobs" section on Craigslist and other sites often.

An ad appeared from a Realty organization looking for people interested in being trained to be a Realtor. In fact, the cost of the training would be reimbursable if you signed up with them after getting licensed! I was very interested in this; I had always loved looking at houses. I had once considered real estate but was told that you really needed to have six months' financial cushion because it could take that long to make a sale. At that time (probably 15 years prior) we didn't have that freedom. I loved research, and this I could do part-time, so I could still work on the book!

I still had concerns, as I did have enough spiritual awareness to realize that I could be deceived into thinking this was God's will when it might very well be my own desires. I didn't have the insight into my dilemma yet, or at least I wasn't willing to admit it. However, the ad also said you could change your mind within a 30-day period and get your money back! It seemed perfect to at least try it out. I prayed that if I was deceived, if it wasn't God's will, for Him to make it plain and shut the door. I had learned enough in my walk to at least do that!

I talked to my husband, my kids, and my Christian friends. They all thought it was a good idea, that it made sense. My kids were a little hesitant because it would take away from my time with them and the grandkids, but I assured them I could manage it all. So, I responded to the ad and began the coursework and in-person weekly trainings. I asked repeatedly if it was possible to do it part-time and was assured that yes, absolutely, many agents are part-time. I continued to pray.

On the third week, as I was reading about all the footwork required the first year – the canvassing of neighborhoods, putting flyers everywhere, probability of 500 contacts before the first sale, etc., I began to have some doubts about the part-time idea, certainly at first. I could sense the reality that I would be probably very involved, perhaps bordering on obsessed at first (knowing my personality and desire for excellence in everything I do). As I was contemplating these things, I heard the Holy Spirit whisper, "Oh, so you are willing to put all this time and money into Real Estate, but not into the book I gave you?" OUCH! Wow! Okay, then. All done!

Much to my surprise, Holy Spirit then reminded me of the "It's Time" word again. Oh dear. How could I have forgotten that? How could my husband have forgotten that? My kids? Wow! What a wake-up call. I can't help but think, what if I'd gone all the way with it? I could have been out on a call and gotten into a head-on collision! Thank God for His leading, for the still, small voice of the Holy Spirit, and for His lessons in my life!

I Do Not Change

My words are eternal and I do not change;
Your circumstances I arrange
To bring forth an expected end,
My Spirit searches; My words He will tend.

My plans for you are good, you will see;
You are being shaped for eternity.
You have seen Me lifted on high;
A lesser walk will not satisfy

Stay in the Light and Keep Moving Forward

Early summer 2016 was a tumultuous time of unrest in my soul as I focused a lot of time and energy on the writing of this book. Many things were being revisited that had caused me a lot of pain. Doubt and fear were ever present. I wanted to quit.

During a time of seeking, I received a vision where I was in a large company of people on a journey. I could see many ahead of me, and there were many more behind – men, women, and children. We were moving toward a distant vista that was glowing in amber, as if through a lens of clear honey. The golden light illuminated everything, from the vegetation near the path we were on to the varied shades of green in the hills beyond. The colors were vibrant and intense, much more than I have ever seen in the natural. Everything had a cast of golden light upon it, and the light towards which we were walking was magnetic in its beauty, rich and radiant. We were walking on the ridgeline of an elevation; to our left was a deep valley, on the right a steep ravine and towering cliffs on the other side. We were focused and intent, not hurriedly rushing, but walking with purpose towards the destination.

I heard a sound, a rumbling vibration. The sound began to build in intensity and I became aware that it was the thundering of a multitude of horses running. I looked to the left, into the valley. As far as my eyes could see were armies upon armies advancing toward us, dark horses carrying riders in dark robes, with faces covered by dark hoods. The riders carried long spears with razor-sharp tips upheld. The horses were creating great clouds of dust over the valley. Looking ahead, I saw that there was no darkness where we were headed; in fact, the light seemed intensified. I began to feel fear when I looked at the armies advancing toward us. Some of the others in our company were starting to run and scream; as they ran, they fell. Others tripped over them, also falling to the ground, causing more wounding and delays.

I heard, **"Do not fear. Stay in the light. If you stay in the light and continue moving with Me, I will take you to your destination. In My light, the enemy cannot touch you. Darkness cannot enter the light. Light dispels darkness. Stay in the light."**

The armies drew closer, and they began to race up the mountain toward us. When they began to get near, it was as if a magnetic force repelled them and they fell backwards, plunging to the ground and destroying each other in frustration.

Do not fear. Stay in the light. Keep moving forward.

"Then Jesus said unto them, Yet a little while is the light with you. Walk hile ye have the light, lest darkness come upon you: for he that walketh in darkness knoweth not whither he goeth." John 12:35 (KJV)

The Great I Am

You are the great
I AM.
You were,
before all time began.

There is nothing hidden from your sight,
We can trust You will bring forth right.
All things are in your hands
And will be in accordance with your plans.

We need not fear,
You are God of all.
Worldly kingdoms will rise
And worldly kingdoms will fall.

Your kingdom is eternal
And soon all will know;
As it is in heaven,
It shall be on the earth below.

The Voice of Distrust

One of the most significant things that was exposed and uprooted from my soul was a root of distrust. The Lord revealed to me that my "agendas" and "planning" were idols. In fact, He told me that my desire for projects and lists, my keeping busy and my life full, was a lack of trust and an idol of control. I was appalled and offended, reminding God of my ability to manage so many projects, with excellence, was something He had given me. In fact, I felt it was the very best part of who I am/was. He told me that that "gift" was for the last season and would not serve me in what He was bringing me into. SELAH. He began to show me times I had missed opportunities because I was "too busy" with my lists of things to do. Sometimes they were ministries! More often, they were things that I had taken on without consulting Him. I was convicted when I realized that much of my life, up to that point, was spent relying on my own desires and thoughts, only consulting Him when it was a crisis or a big decision.

In a conference I attended in the summer of 2016, one of the speakers shared how God had broken through in his life and healed him of a deep wound of distrust. The healing came through great financial loss and his biggest fear coming true – loss of financial security. Through that loss, God showed him that His grace in each day was all that he needed. Over time, God blessed him over and above everything he lost. God also used his experience to bring healing to many others' wounds through an interweaving of circumstances that could only have been wrought through God's hands. It deeply ministered to me, as that very week God had been orchestrating circumstances in my life to show me my lack of trust in a key area. I broke, and allowed Holy Spirit to minister to me. The following weeks I had other opportunities to trust God in this area and can honestly say, Praise God, this time I passed the tests!

Trust is a key issue with many layers and levels. We may trust God in certain areas and not others. In early 2017, my husband and I took a trip set apart for a time of consecrated seeking. I had some fear arise and the Lord took me into a deep wound from childhood based on experiences I had where, in a perfect world, my parents would have protected me from danger.

This formed a belief that I had no one to protect me from danger and I had to protect myself. In my rational mind, I knew that was false, and in fact God had placed many people around me and protected me in my life over and over again. He has shown Himself faithful so many times. Yet when a situation arose that I could not control, where something bad *could* happen, fear came in boldly. The Holy Spirit took me into childhood memories where I realized that the fear was based on times my parents should have protected me and didn't. I had to release tears of pain and fear and allow Holy Spirit to bring the healing comfort of God in the reality of Jesus Christ's presence, so that I could be in a place of full trust once again.

Trust Me

Do you trust enough to fully let go?
If fear is arising, you must say no,
The Father's love will not let me fall
His eyes are on me; he waits for my call.

He will allow me to falter and fail
To show me that my works cannot avail
or bring me to that place of rest,
Only in Him, am I fully blessed.

This comes from trusting the Father's plan,
Seeing my name on the palm of his hand,
Letting Him lead me
To the Promised Land.

It is an unfamiliar place;
Unsettling to swim in a sea of grace,
Led only by desire
To see His face,

Willing to live in a transitional space
Where boundaries of time are erased,
My essence of being in His embrace;
His love the tether of my constraints.

In early 2016, Kerry had a prophetic dream. In the dream he was in a large industrial building/factory setting being shown around by the boss of the company. The sense was that he was applying for a job. It was an assembly plant of some sort. The boss was showing him what was being produced there. There were large rectangular electronic parts that were to be fitted into a larger piece.

The job was not something he had applied for, but there was an undercurrent of favor where he was brought into this setting. He hadn't planned on it or applied for it, nor was he qualified at all for that type of work. There were innuendos that Kerry would get the job, but the boss couldn't come out and tell him that because he was "in training" and it depended on his willingness to go through the process. In the dream, the boss said, "You will be *able* to do this and it is a seven-week training." Kerry understood that if he was *willing* to complete the training, the job would be his, but it was up to Kerry whether or not he *accepted* the assignment and *completed* the training.

So after Kerry had this dream, it was obvious it was prophetic in nature, and that it was a process/training/testing period Kerry would be in (7 weeks) until the completion, when Kerry would be set in place in this new thing God was bringing about. We thought perhaps advancement at work, or fulfillment of a different dream Kerry had some time ago about ministry, or something else, but clearly something significant.

A few months later, one morning when Kerry got up, God spoke to him and said, **"I have given you the fourth gift."** Kerry looked up the different areas in the Bible that talk about spiritual gifts and felt confirmation that it was authority for exhortation/edification.

Soon after, Kerry heard in his spirit Deuteronomy 25:17-19, and it was applicable to a spirit of passivity that Kerry had been battling his whole life. In the text, Amalek attacked the weaker part of the camp that was lagging. Kerry sensed that God was removing the openness to being feeble-minded, faint and weary and Kerry's *letting* the spirit of Amalek oppress him. He heard God say, "The remembrance of Amalek will be blotted out." This was specific to the section in the dream about training. His training was essential for the work of the ministry, in learning perseverance. In the months to come Kerry was aware that he was being tested in the Golden Vessels ministry (the ministry we founded together and serve in), and in the workplace.

Subsequently, there were numerous things that happened in the workplace and in our lives that led us to intensely seek God in prayer for direction as to the timing of Kerry's eventual retirement from full-time work. I had been heavily burdened about it, and feeling we really needed to seek the Lord, that the timing was at hand, yet being careful to discern by the spirit and not soulish desire (desires rooted in the mind, will and emotions versus hearing Holy Spirit). We wanted to be sure of the leading of the Lord.

For some months, and building in intensity, I had been feeling very strongly the need to get away and be alone with God, or with Kerry coming also, to write and to seek God. As the end of the year drew near, I sensed an urgency that we seek the Lord for direction (over and above the writing assignment). I sensed it was very significant in timing, that it had to be the end of 2016/beginning of 2017.

Monday night, Nov. 28, I put out a fleece (Judges 6:36-40) to determine if I was hearing correctly from the Lord. I prayed that if it was His will for Kerry to retire, that He would show me by the end of the week with money from an unexpected source. I wrote it down so I could show it to Kerry when the prayer was answered.

Three days later I received an email from a friend of Kerry's who we rarely talk with as he lives out of state. He said his wife was reading "Moses — Shocked in the Desert" and could not put it down. They wanted to purchase a large quantity for Christmas presents. Wow; I was astounded! This was clearly money from an unexpected source. Holy Spirit reminded me that the very first purchase of my book was from an unexpected source and He told me then that this is how it would be.

I told Kerry about the prayer/fleece, my note, and the email. He said he wanted to put out a second fleece. His fleece was the same, money from an unexpected source, by Sunday. Later that night and he told me that the previous day the Holy Spirit impressed upon him Ecclesiastes 12:11, "*The words of the wise are as goads, and as nails fastened by the masters of assemblies, which are given from one Shepherd."* He was reminded of the dream of the factory assembly job. When he told me this, we became aware of the process of his prophetic edification gift coming forth in preaching the Word at our ministry. Words as goads, nails fashioned by the masters of assemblies, from one Shepherd. Amazing.

Kerry noted the Hebraic month we were in (Cheshvan), and how we had just learned that is a time to listen for divine orders and timing, and being obedient. Also, that it is a month of transformation, and Moses a significant type, noting the correlation of his friend reading and wanting to purchase copies of my book "Moses…"

The next day I received a second email from his friend, who wanted to double the order. I felt God was saying to Kerry, "What, you didn't believe me the first time?"

God is the Master of assembly. He is always in the process of moving us toward His purpose and plan for our lives. It is amazing to me how He uses people, places and things to bring us to an understanding, or an acceptance of His leading, so that we can *know* that He is leading. The world would call it coincidental. When you have eyes to see and ears to hear by the Spirit, (and by the new birth have received the Spirit of Christ), you know better.

Training time is transition time. I had been in transition since 2010, and now Kerry was clearly told that he is also in process of coming forth into Purpose! The vision I received so many years ago (late 1993, before we were married) of us ministering together and the Glory of God being so strong, was in sight!

In spring of 2017, Kerry did retire and our ministry began to expand. The training doesn't end, of course. We are continually being trained by the Spirit of God to move upwards and onward in His purposes. We are propelled by new revelation of the Word into our spirit man that prepares us for each new step and creates the very thing God requires of us. Praise His Name!

Master of Assembly

I am the Master of assembly,
Ever working in your life.
You may not understand My ways,
But I AM with you all your days.

Be still, at peace and you will hear
My voice, for I am always near.
My ways are not your ways, it's true;
Keep close and they may be revealed to you.

The closer you come, the more you will know
I will lead you where you should go;
Moment by moment the way becomes clear
Listen, I am ever near.

Staying Focused on Hearing the One True Voice

The focus of my journey has become staying positioned to hear the One True Voice (the Eternal Voice of God), and walking in obedience so that His voice becomes clearer. The challenge is always to balance family, ministry, and personal interests. It is a continual seeking, listening, identifying my thoughts and breaking through the oppression and distractions that come to hinder me from fulfilling my calling.

> *"For though we walk in the flesh, we do not war according to the flesh. For the weapons of our warfare are not carnal but mighty in God for pulling down strongholds, casting down arguments and every high thing that exalts itself against the knowledge of God, bringing every thought into captivity to the obedience of Christ..." 2* Corinthians 10:3-5 (KJV)

A few years ago I looked up obedience in the Strong's Concordance and was shocked to find that in this verse the word obedience means "attentive hearkening!"[1] Think of that and how it changes the meaning of the verse! I always thought it meant trying to remember what Jesus had said and then rebuking the lies, and we certainly have to do that. However, "attentive hearkening of Christ" means that I have to be still, at peace, listening for His voice. I have to pierce through whatever clouds of doubt and lying voices are thundering and listen closely so that I can hear the still, small voice of the Spirit in that moment. Very different, and actually simpler, though not simple by any means when you are under an onslaught mentally or emotionally.

There are always challenges in life – family, finances, health, etc. Daily I face my own fleshly or soulish desires that war against the Spirit of God within me. Some may be wondering what I mean by "soulish." God created us spirit, soul and body. Spirit is the part of us that communicates with God. Our soul is our mind, will and emotions. Body is obvious. What helps me understand the difference is I think of the soul as what we are born with - our genetics, predispositions. After that, everything that happens in our lives is absorbed and becomes our soul, like a sponge. Our "spirit" man is built through the

Word of God, prayer, fellowship with other believers, obedience to God's voice/impression/conscience. What we hear by the Spirit of God, through our born-again spirit, is often very different from what our "natural" man (soulish) wants or hears. The Scofield reference Bible talks about the natural man versus spiritual versus carnal. The way I understand it, the differentiating factor between natural and carnal is that the natural man isn't born again so is living all that he knows to do, acting "naturally." The carnal man is one who is born again but is choosing to live carnally, or out of his fleshly/soulish desires.

Sometimes I am not as successful in this area as I would like to be. In late fall of 2016, God revealed a pattern that it was time to break. I had three ministry engagements within a four-week period. The first was a last-minute opportunity that required travel, the second took nearly a month of preparation (I was able to use the plane flights and layover for some of that), the third was sharing my testimony, which was the fifth time I've done that in a three-year period. After the first engagement, I had a health issue arise. I am familiar with spiritual attacks and backlash, so I wasn't surprised. However, some of it lingered and required visits to specialists. I noticed myself toying with backing off, and realized there was a backing off pattern after breakthrough and victory, or intense ministry. I was reminded of what the Lord says in Hebrews 10:38, *"Now the just shall live by faith; But if anyone **draws back**, My soul has no pleasure in him."*

So, what are/were the thoughts causing the drawing back? Thoughts along the line of, "I need a break." I justify this with the physical reality that we all need rest after exertion. There is a reality to needing to take care of our bodies, to being a good and wise steward. Yet I have to be aware of my own patterns, those soulish inclinations and devilish attacks that seek to hinder my going forward. You might ask, "Well why would you not want to go forward? You certainly know from your experience that there is no satisfaction in being stagnant; in fact, there is no settling, that is an illusion. If you aren't going forward you are moving backward." I counsel myself this way. I have to move forward. Yet there is a fine line; when I am in transition and unsure of where He is leading, I don't want to go forward in the works of the flesh, leaning on my own understanding. In waiting periods, I have learned not to get out of His timing.

I heard the Lord saying:

Preparation

It is a time of rest,
A time of seeking,
For there is more coming
That will be for my keeping.

I am being prepared for an elevation,
I will need to hear and see new revelation.
The heights and depths will be plumbed anew;
This is what I am being called into.

Seek My face, and don't look back,
Recognize when there is an attack.
Yet keep moving forward, do not stand still,
You must stay in My perfect will.

The time is coming when you will see
What it means to be truly free.
Keep yourself unentangled, untethered
From the works of the flesh or soulish endeavors.

All bondages
Must be severed.
There are storms coming
That must be weathered.

To me alone
You must be yoked,
That my anointing remain upon,
As a cloak.

You will go here and there, as bidden.
I will show you treasures, aforeto hidden.
Stay alert, be ready to move
My presence in you will soon be proved.

The Eternal Voice

The Author of Eternity

He sends one here, He sends one there;
It seems so happenstance.
Yet in His glorious, purposeful grace
There is nothing left to chance.

He sees all things, He knows all things,
He works them all together,
And by His power they are held,
There is nothing that can sever;
He is the Author of forever.

The Eternal Voice and My Story

You may be wondering why I segued from my story into "The Eternal Voice." Remember, the focal point in my telling this story is one of my journey from confusion to clarity. Although I am no longer in confusion with a cacophony of voices clamoring for my attention, there is still the daily process of staying "rightly tuned" in my hearing.

As I move forward into God's purposes, trusting Him and being obedient, I receive greater clarity and understanding than I have ever had, and the clearer I hear and see, the more that God gives me. I am using this section of the book to share with you, the reader, some of the ways in which Holy Spirit speaks to me. Why? To encourage you to continue to press forward towards God, provide tools to assist in the journey, and wisdom that I have learned about the One who inhabits Eternity and how we relate to Him. I exhort you to do all that you can to make your calling and election sure. Press toward the mark. There is a high calling and nothing in this world compares to His Presence.

The truth is, the Eternal Voice — God — the Source of all life, Creator and Sustainer — has been wooing me my whole life, but I didn't know it. Even when I was into "New Age" there was the false, luring me to destruction, while at the same time my Loving Father was drawing me, only allowing me to go so far before revealing the false foundation where I was headed. Looking to men, wanting the voice of love and approval, of identity, finding none of them to satisfy, was one. Looking to other avenues for identity all came to the same end. The same voice that spoke the world into existence speaks to me of my eternal identity in Him.

His "voice" resonates deep within my being. His voice is the voice of Truth. It may not be an audible voice (in fact, rarely is audible), but it is a "knowing," a bearing witness in the depths of my being that cannot be denied. Though I ran the other direction and made my bed in hell, I could not escape.

> "Whither shall I go from thy spirit? or whither shall I flee
> from thy presence? If I ascend up into heaven, thou art there:
> if I make my bed in hell, behold, thou art there. If I take the

wings of the morning, and dwell in the uttermost parts of the sea; Even there shall thy hand lead me, and thy right hand shall hold me. If I say, Surely the darkness shall cover me; even the night shall be light about me. Yea, the darkness hideth not from thee; but the night shineth as the day: the darkness and the light are both alike to thee." Psalms 139:7-12 (KJV)

Now, at this time in my life, my goal and desire is to be one with Him. He is my true love — Eternal Love — my home, my identity, my source, and my fulfillment. I AM HIS. I always was and always will be.

My Eternal Home

Heaven is my eternal home.
No matter how far I roam
The Father
Will never leave me alone.

Ever present,
He draws me near,
Even when
I can't see or hear.

No, I don't spend my days sitting in a closet contemplating Him. He has created me to be a part of His Body in the earth, ministering in accordance to the gifts He has given me and the calling that He has on my life. I have a family I love, friends, and fellow laborers in the Kingdom. I have a house to maintain, and a garden to tend. I am so aware of the honor and privilege of my role as wife, mother of two beautiful daughters, and grandmother to five precious grandchildren. It is a blessing to be able to impart gifts and wisdom into those that I love so dearly, and to enjoy and receive what they bring to my life!

Yet the context from which I live and function as a wife, mother, grandmother, friend, and fellow laborer in Kingdom purposes, is to recognize the incredible gift of life and purpose, live fully engaged in every relationship, living my life with purpose – to please Him and that others would see Him, know Him, be reconciled to Him and be fully aligned to His purpose; **to be His voice in the earth.**

I enjoy the blessing of family, friends, and the opportunity to minister with and to others. My goal is to be aware of divine opportunities that present themselves as I engage in life, in the normal, "humdrum" duties of shopping, running errands, etc.

For this is where He often speaks – to me or through me – in the realm of relationship with others. I can easily be a hermit, but I become dissatisfied, moroseful, negative, inwardly focused. We are created to engage with others. An essential element of "Body" life is the interworking of all the parts (Ephesians 4:16), just as our brain functions in the natural, directing all the parts, each interacting with the other. Yet we have free will – we have to choose to engage with others and learn to get along, to interact in love, recognizing that He is love and allowing His love to rule our hearts and minds. For extroverts, it's easier to engage, although there are other challenges such as ego and pride. Introverts like me have to make an effort, push ourselves, yet also recognize that we get depleted from engaging with others and need to replenish our supply. Truly, the challenge for all is to continue to stay focused on our Source and letting Him lead and guide!

Walking in eternal identity requires focus and intent. It takes discipline and prioritization of time to ensure that I am continuing to walk in cadence with

God. Rest assured, God has His ways to ensure that this happens, but how much easier it is when I will to do His will. Sometimes God reveals things to me by the Spirit, in visions and/or dreams, to keep me moving forward. I am sharing some of these with you to encourage you on your journey. The reality is that when things are revealed by Holy Spirit, they are prophetic realities that are eternally true.

> *"That which hath been is now; and that which is to be hath already been; and God requireth that which is past."* Ecclesiastes 3:15 (KJV)

So this section is focused more on the Eternal Voice and what I hear Him say. I believe that which He speaks is timeless. Some of the things may not be relevant to you at the specific time you are reading them, but I believe they will be at some point. We go through cycles in our Christian walk and we are ever ascending in the cycles. Often I have to go back and remember these things to encourage myself to continue to press on. Other times, revelation may be necessary to enlighten momentary darkness that has come from walking in the flesh or from the attacks of the enemy.

If you are a person who has a gift of "seeing" or "hearing" but it has been perverted by the enemy throughout your life, or shut down by those who don't understand, I pray that the truth of purpose and destiny will be stirred to activation as you read the things revealed to me by the Holy Spirit.

Come Forth!

Ears be opened to hear
The Voice!
Spirit man —
Rise and rejoice!

Eyes be opened to Reality;
See and hear - be set free -
To walk in eternal destiny.
Come forth, true identity!

The Eternal is a Joyful Sound

I am sharing the following because it was a significant event in my life. I struggled with where to place this in the book. Over the years, as I have recalled it and given it more thought, I realized that it was the first time that I had an awareness of the Eternal Voice in the sense of actually having an ongoing conversation with God in the middle of a vision. I received this in 2013, the day after a glorious gathering of prophetic and apostolic people. I was stirred to "do something different" in my seeking of the Lord. I went into a different room, determined not to leave until I heard something. I received far more than I ever expected, and what I received was life-changing. This was truly the "Eternal Voice" taking me on a journey that exposed me to a reality that I had previously only had glimpses of before.

I was reading the word, and saw in Psalms 89:15-16, *"Blessed is the people that know the joyful sound: they shall walk, O LORD, in the light of thy countenance. In thy name shall they rejoice all the day: and in thy righteousness shall they be exalted."*

I began meditating on the blessing of the joyful sound and that it is His name that causes my heart to rejoice. From that point, my spirit poured out to God and I received from Him. I have italicized what I said to Him. His responses to me are bolded and in quotations.

> *Your Name is the joyful sound. The sound of your voice makes melody in my heart. My soul desires you. I desire to hear your voice, O Lord my God.*
>
> *I desire to hear your voice; the sound to which my soul does rejoice. At your Name does my heart sing and my life becomes an offering. I long to give myself to you, for you have proven yourself to be true. There is no other voice I hear that pulls my soul to be ever near.*
>
> *You alone are my heart's desire; you fan the flame with your Holy Fire. My soul comes alive as I feel your presence; my spirit responds*

with Holy Reverence.

Awake, awake, my soul and sing, in awe and wonder at your King. I lift my eyes within your grace, to look upon your lovely face; to take your hand and come away, my Beloved, with you today.

My time with you is precious gold, overflowing with love untold. I wake before the dawn draws near, to wait until your voice I hear.

"Daughter, my love, come away with me, let My spirit set you free. Ride the high places of eternity; there are things you need to see."

"In My heart are depths of grace, that I long for you to taste. Feast at My table, have your fill, that you may go forth and fulfill My will."

"Wait on Me, My tender one, I have much that must be done. Wait on Me, do not hasten to leave; to My bosom you must cleave."

"Let Me hold you close, My love, My tender one, My sweet, My dove."

"Feel My heart beat; to Me be attuned. It takes time to heal your wound."

"Let Me restore you and make you whole, in the deep places of your soul."

"Touch Me, partake, be with Me. This is the place you need to be."

"Open your eyes and look upon Me. Look into My piercings, what do you see?"

I gaze into eternity, forever with you I will be. I see a land far and wide; I see myself by your side, walking, hand in hand are we. I see a night sky filled with stars and one great star, magnificent and bright, lighting up the darkest night.

"This is My light, shining for you. Stay focused on me, with My light you will shine. There are others I am drawing to be Mine."

"Ride the high places of the earth, there are visions in you that must be birthed. Stay close to Me and you will see visions of eternity."

"Speak forth My words that you have heard me say. They bring forth power for the day, and vision to take you on the way."

"I will show you the way; you must stay near. You must be able My voice to hear. I will light the path and make it clear."

> I can see the path and it is clear, though off to the sides there are things that bring fear. There are storms in the shadows as dark as night, but the path I see is bright by Your light. If I see danger, my eyes have strayed. I look back at You and see the path You have made. Help me to keep my eyes focused on You, that unto You I will be true.

I left the room to share these things with Kerry. As I read them out loud, another piece came in an open vision. I saw this as a transparency over what exists in the natural. I was in a beautiful land, rolling hills golden green and lit up all around in a glowing amber light. I saw the path with the Lord bright and clear, a wide path, though on the sides of the path were darkness, storms, visions of hell; not off the sides looking down the path where He is taking me, but the sides next to me, off the path I am on with Him. I see myself joyous, laughing, holding His hand. As we walk, others are drawn to us and trying to rise up. Some need help. I see Him reaching out His hand to one, then I follow His leading and reach out my hand to another one. One only has enough strength to raise an index finger. I grab the finger and the Lord holds on to me and gives me strength to pull the man out.

Multitudes are now coming and following. I see one covered with filth, like muck from a swamp. As He gazes upon her, the filth begins to drip off her; He continues to gaze upon her until it all has come off and she is now bright. I hear, *"Kings shall come to the brightness of thy rising."* (Isaiah 60:3, paraphrased)

This was an amazing pivotal event, one in which I remind myself often of His incredible love, and the eternal reality which is so much more real to me than the material world where we spend most of our time. Staying in His rest so that we can hear His voice and stay aligned to His purposes is the focus of my life, and Kerry's, at this time.

Revealing of Purpose through Eternal Reality

In the process of writing this book, there have been a number of things that the Lord revealed to me about my purpose and how He has been working to that end throughout my whole life.

When I started writing "Moses – Shocked in the Desert" in 2007, one of the first scriptures given was Isaiah 55:3, *"Incline your ear and come to me; hear and your soul shall live; and I will make an everlasting covenant with you – the sure mercies of David."* This scripture takes me directly into His presence even now. Little did I know how significant this scripture would become for me.

On the eve of Rosh Hashana, September 2015 (Hebraic year 5776), I received a vision in a dream about the sure mercies of David. I saw a dark night sky, purplish-blue and inky looking with little flecks of white here and there, like wave tips or dull stars. Then a door appeared in the upper right area, filled with illumination of light, glory shining through. Next a burnished gold key appeared in the left portion. Last, I heard these words as they were written in gold as I heard them spoken, ***"I have given you the sure mercies of David."*** I woke up, stunned. I had never before received a vision in a dream and it felt so pregnant with significance.

I looked up scriptures regarding these things, and there were a few that I felt strong confirmation about. The first and strongest was Revelation 3:7-12,

> *"And to the angel of the church in Philadelphia write; These things saith he that is holy, he that is true, he that hath the key of David, he that openeth, and no man shutteth; and shutteth, and no man openeth; I know thy works: behold, I have set before thee an open door, and no man can shut it: for thou hast a little strength, and hast kept my word, and hast not denied my name. Behold, I will make them of the synagogue of Satan, which say they are Jews, and are not, but do lie; behold, I will make them to come and worship before thy feet, and to know that I have loved thee. Because thou hast kept the word of my patience, I also will keep thee from*

the hour of temptation, which shall come upon all the world, to try them that dwell upon the earth. Behold, I come quickly: hold that fast which thou hast, that no man take thy crown. Him that overcometh will I make a pillar in the temple of my God, and he shall go no more out: and I will write upon him the name of my God, and the name of the city of my God, which is new Jerusalem, which cometh down out of heaven from my God: and I will write upon him my new name."

I wept when I read this. Only God knew how I needed to hear this, and how significant this was for me. He had been telling me that He would open doors for me. I looked up "strength" and it is the dunamis power that performs miracles. I have a "little" in that sometimes He uses me in others receiving healings. And God knows I keep His word. His word has become life and breath to me. The Word of God creates the life of Christ in us. It separates the soul from the spirit. It is my lifeblood. Also, He has shown me His patience and longsuffering and I do testify of that, for sure. I have learned patience over the years while waiting for His perfect timing (learned from not doing that) and His sovereignty in my life. And I have not denied His Name (His authority) in my life. His name is the name above ALL names; all things are subject to Him, and in Him all things exist and have their being. He also knew that one of my biggest fears has been going through the tribulation. Here He *gave me* assurance that He would keep me from this. I didn't go looking for this and claiming it, He *gave* it to me in a vision in a dream.

Other scriptures are significant to this vision: Isaiah 22:22,

> *"And the key of the house of David will I lay upon his shoulder; so he shall open, and none shall shut; and he shall shut, and none shall open."*

In Psalms 89:20-37, (the same chapter of "The Joyful Sound") I found what this covenant means:

> *"I have found David my servant; with my holy oil have I anointed him: With whom my hand shall be established: mine arm also shall strengthen him. The enemy shall not*

exact upon him; nor the son of wickedness afflict him. And I will beat down his foes before his face, and plague them that hate him. But my faithfulness and my mercy shall be with him: and in my name shall his horn be exalted. I will set his hand also in the sea, and his right hand in the rivers. He shall cry unto me, Thou art my father, my God, and the rock of my salvation. Also I will make him my firstborn, higher than the kings of the earth. My mercy will I keep for him for evermore, and my covenant shall stand fast with him. **His seed also will I make to endure for ever, and his throne as the days of heaven. If his children forsake my law, and walk not in my judgments; if they break my statutes, and keep not my commandments; then will I visit their transgression with the rod, and their iniquity with stripes. Nevertheless my lovingkindness will I not utterly take from him, nor suffer my faithfulness to fail. My covenant will I not break, nor alter the thing that is gone out of my lips.** *Once have I sworn by my holiness that I will not lie unto David. His seed shall endure forever, and his throne as the sun before me. It shall be established for ever as the moon, and as a faithful witness in heaven. Selah."*

Certainly, not the least is Isaiah 55:3, one of the key verses in my book "Moses...."

> *"Incline your ear, and come unto me: hear, and your soul shall live; and I will make an everlasting covenant with you, even the* **sure mercies of David.***"*

Are you kidding me? See? God was really bringing it on home for me, His covenant with me and His purpose for my life. He is so good! I am nobody; seek Him and you will also find out how good He is!

Also, I realized recently, that for years, I had one of those corkboard hotplates imprinted with a picture of a path and the scripture, Ps. 25:4, *"Show me your ways, O Lord; teach me your paths."*

This is what "Moses..." is all about, and all the ways of the Lord (that He showed me through the book) lead to fulfillment of His purpose for our lives. He gave me the answer to my dilemma, my big life question of "What is the purpose of Life?"

Our Wounds Transformed by His Glory
(Become an Integral Part of Our Eternal Story)

Bear with me a few moments as I revisit an "old section" of my life, as it has been transformed by His Glory. God has revealed greater purpose in my life through the transformation of wounds.

When I was writing out the section about the sexual molestation and the subsequent beliefs about my identity that formed from that experience, God brought to my remembrance the moment when my mom came in. I became very aware of "self" and ashamed of my body. How I looked became paramount to me in the value that I placed on myself. I would ask my mom, "Am I pretty?" She would say, "Pretty is as pretty does." Well, I knew that I was doing bad things, so therefore I wasn't pretty.

When I saw a picture of myself at around age 8, and I was pudgy and one of my legs was bowed (the one that had the congenital defect), I hated myself. Prior to that, I don't think I was really consciously aware of how I looked. When I was overweight, I was unattractive in my own eyes. My self-perception was that I had little worth or value, and would not be desirable to others. The other parts of my being, outside the physical body, had not been affirmed in my early years (to my remembrance...perhaps the wounds were too deep to let it in as it would have messed with my belief that I didn't matter and I was crazy, something was wrong with me).

This voice recurred in every romantic relationship. When the "feeling of being desired" wore off, or I felt unattractive, I was very open to admiration from others. I had no idea who I was, the formation of my identity was based on wounds versus who God created me to be. I know that many people have no idea who they are, and this is now a passion for me – for others to know who God created them to be.

People don't even realize how destructive it is when we focus on our "creation" versus the "Creator" (Romans 1:20-25). The enemy used this deceptive tool with Eve in the garden, insinuating she had a "lack." This brought doubt to God's word and the focus onto self, and implied God had an evil motive. Now the lie penetrates to self, in the form of self-awareness, self-exaltation, and self-pleasing.

> "Now the serpent was more subtle than any beast of the field which the LORD God had made. And he said unto the woman, Yea, hath God said, Ye shall not eat of every tree of the garden? And the woman said unto the serpent, We may eat of the fruit of the trees of the garden: But of the fruit of the tree which is in the midst of the garden, God hath said, Ye shall not eat of it, neither shall ye touch it, lest ye die. And the serpent said unto the woman, Ye shall not surely die: For God doth know that in the day ye eat thereof, then your eyes shall be opened, and ye shall be as gods, knowing good and evil. And when the woman saw that the tree was good for food, and that it was pleasant to the eyes, and a tree to be desired to make one wise, she took of the fruit thereof, and did eat, and gave also unto her husband with her; and he did eat. And the eyes of them both were opened, and they knew that they were naked; and they sewed fig leaves together, and made themselves aprons." Genesis 3:1-7 (KJV)

See the focus? It's on self!

Now, my initial wounds occurred when I was a child. I did not bring them onto myself; they were wounds to my identity from others, those in authority over me. Yet, in the fullness of time, after multiple relationships were destroyed, and I nearly was in the process, God began pulling away the veils of lies so that I could be healed and restored, aligned to His purposes for my life as He built me up with His Word and Spirit into His identify for me.

> "For I know the thoughts that I think toward you, saith the LORD, thoughts of peace, and not of evil, to give you an expected end." Jeremiah 29:11 (KJV)

> "And we know that all things work together for good to them that love God, to them who are the called according to his purpose." Romans 8:28 (KJV)

God is forming a new identity in me, the one that He created for me from the beginning. It is He who is at work in me. Oh, there is a submission to His plans that must take place; we have to be willing to let Him have His way in our lives, but in His grace and mercy and goodness, He will not leave us alone! His eye is always on His purpose, He sees the end from the beginning and calls forth those things that be not as though they are (Romans 4:17). When we begin to perceive this, it propels us forward. We begin to hear with the ears of the Spirit within us and hope is created. The vision is cast from the throne room of Heaven, spoken into the fertile ground of our hearts (furrowed from life's circumstances) where it begins to take root. The Lord knows who are His.

> *"Nevertheless the foundation of God standeth sure, having this seal, The Lord knoweth them that are his. And, Let every one that nameth the name of Christ depart from iniquity."* 2 Timothy 2:19 (KJV)

What is iniquity? In the original language in the New Testament, it means: fault, iniquity, mischief, punishment of iniquity, sin. In the Old Testament, the meaning is perversity, i.e. (moral) evil -- fault, iniquity, mischief, punishment (of iniquity), sin; also, to do amiss, bow down, make crooked, commit iniquity, pervert, do perversely, trouble, turn.

What the Lord speaks to me in this is that the difference between iniquity and sin, especially in speaking of generational iniquity, is that iniquity causes to make crooked, to turn away into another path that is intended to pervert the plan of God. Sin is to bear the brunt, or guilt; to miss the mark. One seems more intentional, our individual moments where we choose sin. Perhaps continued sinning creates a stronghold that roots deep and causes the crooked path that is a potential hazard for future generations.

These wounds can be healed and the places Christ transforms us, the generational iniquitous root can be broken as we enter into Covenant with Him. In fact, these wounds can become a portal of His Glory to shine through!

I have had two incredible experiences of this truth. The first time, I was having lunch with a friend who was moving away from San Diego. I thought we were just going to have a chat to catch up on our lives before she left, and enjoy fellowship together. I wasn't expecting this to be a ministry opportunity, just a lunch between friends, so I certainly hadn't fasted for it and wasn't even "prayed up" and anticipating God to speak. Just "lunch with a friend" was my thought. So, as we were sharing what had been going on in our lives, I told her that as I had spent the summer months working on this book, God had revealed some amazing things to me about His weaving together things in my life even before I was a Christian. I shared with her that as a teenager I wrestled with the whole "What's life about anyway, what's the purpose" question, and that the culmination of "Moses – Shocked in the Desert" was God's purpose for our lives! He gave me the answer! He also instilled a desire in my heart for others to receive revelation of purpose.

I also shared with her that when my daughters were teenagers I had a hotplate on the table that had a beautiful photo of an illuminated path through trees, with the scripture, *"Show me your ways, O Lord; teach me your paths." Psalms 25:4 (KJV)* I added that God reminded me of this as I wrote, and the correlation with "Moses..." being about learning God's ways (His paths)!

I shared with her that Holy Spirit had begun revealing how not only does God work all things together for our good (Romans 8:28), but when we submit our wounds to Him and allow Him to come into those places, they are filled with His Glory, and those very wounds become a portal for His Glory to pour into others. As I said this, it was as if a lightning bolt came down onto our table and I heard and felt the magnitude of its force. She shook tremendously and began weeping uncontrollably and I felt the shaking myself. The glory of God came in waves upon us, and it was as if there was no one else in the crowded restaurant except us. She looked at me and the fire of God was in her eyes, and she said, "I am taking this to my sister and this will transform her life." She and her sisters share a similar background of childhood wounds. It was amazing. God shocked me like He never had, literally!

The next time I shared it with another person who has a similar story, almost the exact same thing happened. Not the lightning bolt experience for me, but she felt something hit her and she began shaking and weeping, and received impartation of LIFE. God showed me that what He had revealed to me in the Spirit was TRUTH; when it is received by those with ears to hear by the Spirit, this Glory is imparted to them in that same area.

During this time is also when God gave me deeper revelation to the reality of Him working all things together for good. He reminded me of Joseph's journey, all his struggles and pain. In the end, he was able to say, *"But as for you, ye thought evil against me: but God meant it unto good, to bring to pass, as it is this day, to save much people alive."* Genesis 50:20 (KJV)

Filled with His Glory

When we allow the Lord Most High
To enter those places where a part of us died,
He fills us with His glory divine
He says, "Now that you are fully mine,

I take those wounds and make them whole.
My glory has been to you extolled.
Now go, and speak what you have been told
Yes, in my strength you can be bold.

Where the enemy was given reign
In your suffering, in your pain,
This has now become your gain.
My glory has given you a new refrain.

Every vestige of every stain
Removed; My glory will remain.
Go forth and speak, others will hear
They will be set free from pain and fear.

Your words will sink into their ears
My glory will come; all will be clear
I will transform every tear.
Your testimony will be a sharpened spear,

A flaming rod
Filled with fire
Causing others
To come up higher.

The Sound of the Realms of Eternal Glory

When we were in Kauai for our anniversary in 2016, I experienced "hearing the sound" in a profound way. I left the room early in the morning to seek the Lord. I was desperate. We were nearing the end of our trip and I needed to hear Him. Whenever we go to Kauai, the Lord reveals something very significant to me, and I had not heard anything yet this trip. As I walked the grounds, I kept hearing,

> "It is the glory of God to conceal a matter, but the glory of kings is to search out a matter." Proverbs 25:2 (NKJV)

I went to search Him out. The wind had shifted and I felt a shift in the Spirit as well. As I walked, He dropped a heart shaped seed in front of me, a love note.

When I returned to the room, I went to the lanai and sat, staring out at the mountains in the distance and thinking about God's goodness to me, how amazing that He would draw me outside to show me how much He loves me.

> "The LORD hath appeared of old unto me, saying, Yea, I have loved thee with an everlasting love: therefore with lovingkindness have I drawn thee." Jeremiah 31:3 (KJV)

In the distance, I heard a turtledove calling its mate. I turned to Isaiah 55:3,

> "Incline your ear, and come unto me: hear, and your soul shall live; and I will make an everlasting covenant with you, even the sure mercies of David."

I meditated on that, then read the whole chapter. He took me into realms of the spirit and began to speak to me as He showed me things. This poem is an expression of what I heard and saw.

The Everlasting Door

I hear the sound of the turtle dove
Calling unto its mate.
The wind is blowing into my soul,
And I begin to anticipate,

That the Lord, my God, is calling me
To turn aside with Him and see
The heights of Glory on which He soars.
He has opened the everlasting doors.

The King of Glory
He called my name;
Nothing can ever
Be the same.

He bids me, "Come, and be with Me;
I have depths I want you to see -
The realms of beauty beyond compare -
Come with Me, I will take you there.

Let me unfold the fathomless deep
The caverns, my treasuries they keep,
Storehouses full of glories divine;
I give to you from what is mine."

Two turtledoves flew into the lanai and sat at my feet. After a short time, one turned to the other, cooed, and they few off together. I thought on this for a while, amazed at what had transpired, in awe of Him.

I went back into the room to share these incredible things with Kerry. A little later, I laid on the floor to stretch out my muscles; as I turned my head, I saw something under the dresser. I got a long-handled utensil to pull it out. It was a clothespin with "KING" written on it in marker.

> *"It is the glory of God to conceal a matter, but the glory of kings is to search out a matter."* Proverbs. 25:2 (NKJV)

According to Strong's Concordance, glory[2] in the Hebraic language is kabowd, which means weight, splendor, copiousness. The root means to be heavy, rich, glorious — as in the heavy weight of glory. **It is the glory within us that searches the hidden glory of God.**

If you want things handed to you, you will be disappointed; this is not happening! God wants us to *want* Him — to see Him as worth searching out. Yet even if you don't, God in His goodness will work your circumstances to stir up the desire within you to seek after Him. The Apostle Paul's words echo, *"As many as be perfect, be thus minded: and if in anything ye be otherwise minded, God shall reveal even this unto you,"* Philippians 3:15 (KJV). John Robert Stevens, an Apostle during the Latter Rain Movement, said, "God will show you what life is like apart from reaching in to become the sons of God." He has created us with an aching abyss in our hearts, because we are created to be one with Him, carriers of His Glory!

Calling you Forth to the Realms of My Glory

I'm calling you forth
To the realms of my glory.
This is where
You will frame your story.

The enemy seeks
To tear you apart,
Yet I am drawing you
Close to my heart.

So be still and listen
As I call you to me.
I will show you
What I want you to see.

I will set you free
So that you can be with Me.
Immersed in My glory
I AM the frame of your story.

Eternity
(One in the Glory)

Jesus prayed the ultimate prayer for our Glory — and we can be assured that His prayers are *always* answered. In John 17:20-23, we read this:

> "Neither pray I for these alone, but for them also which shall believe on me through their word; That they all may be one; as thou, Father, art in me, and I in thee, that they also may be one in us: that the world may believe that thou hast sent me. And the glory which thou gavest me I have given them; that they may be one, even as we are one: I in them, and thou in me, that they may be made perfect in one; and that the world may know that thou hast sent me, and hast loved them, as thou hast loved me."

What is glory? In the Greek language (the New Testament), the word is "doxa" and some of the meanings are: Where did you get these from?

- splendour, brightness; of the moon, sun, stars
- magnificence, excellence, preeminence, dignity, grace; majesty
- a thing belonging to God; the kingly majesty which belongs to him as supreme ruler, majesty in the sense of the absolute perfection of the deity
- a thing belonging to Christ; the kingly majesty of the Messiah
- the absolutely perfect inward or personal excellency of Christ; the majesty of the angels; as apparent in their exterior brightness
- a most glorious condition, most exalted state; of that condition with God the Father in heaven to which Christ was raised after he had achieved his work on earth
- the glorious condition of blessedness into which is appointed and promised that true Christians shall enter after their Savior's return from heaven

Kingly majesty! Personal excellence! Most exalted state! Glorious condition of blessedness! These are what belong to us! Jesus prayed it, His sanctification in us has this as the appointed end. He is the author and finisher of our salvation (Hebrews 12:2). The finisher of our salvation – implying it is progressive, which we can also see from Hebrews 7:25,

"Wherefore he is able also to save them to the uttermost that come unto God by him, seeing he ever liveth to make intercession for them."

Take heart, wherever you are in your walk with God. Jesus is ever living to make intercession for you, and God is all the while at work in you to will and to do of His good pleasure (Philippians 2:3). Christ in you is the hope of glory (Colossians 1:27). His life in you will accomplish it; it is a done deal, as long as you trust Him and keep moving forward in faith!

When we are walking in continued obedience, maturing in Christ, God raises us up to the place of Kings and Priests. It takes time and training to grow into that role and Jesus living through us. He is both King of Kings and High Priest, so we must be surrendered to Him to be elevated to kingship and priesthood. There is a training for reigning.

"John to the seven churches which are in Asia: Grace be unto you, and peace, from him which is, and which was, and which is to come; and from the seven Spirits which are before his throne; And from Jesus Christ, who is the faithful witness, and the first begotten of the dead, and the prince of the kings of the earth. Unto him that loved us, and washed us from our sins in his own blood, And hath made us kings and priests unto God and his Father; to him be glory and dominion for ever and ever. Amen." (Revelation 1:4-6, KJV)

Your Glory

Your Glory is beyond compare,
More beautiful than jewels so rare.
Dazzling to my mind and soul,
I gaze at You and become whole.

Vision restored,
Hope is made new,
From one moment in time
Spent with You.

"Now may the God of hope fill you with all joy and peace
in believing, that you may abound in hope by the power of
the Holy Spirit." (Romans 15:13)

Created for Him, living in the world; we are in a war and the battle is fierce. What is the purpose? To bring heaven to earth — citizens of the Kingdom, ambassadors for Christ, voices of reconciliation — reconciling others to God. The enemy wants to blindside us, divert us and get us into battles with others to do his dirty work, forgetting that we have a purpose, and that really this is a war between satan and God. Jesus has already won the battle, He has overcome the power of hell, death and the grave, but there are many held captive that do not know the war is over or even that there is a war! They are still trapped in captivity and we have the keys that will set them free. Jesus has given us the keys.

Many times the ways God gives us strategies is through dreams and visions. Remember how I shared the vision in a dream I received about an open door and overcoming? After I received that, some weeks and even months later, many well-known prophets were saying that they had received revelation that we were in an open door time period, that they also heard Isaiah 22:22, or saw a vision of open doors, etc. So that was not just for me!

God gives us encouragement for the Body of Christ. Much of what we who "see" and "hear" receive is not just for us. We are in a time of intense battle, and He has given us the open door for heavenly strategies, open doors for opportunities to advance His kingdom! This is the time!

This is the Time of Restoration

This is the time,
This is the hour,
To have all restored
By the Father's power.

A time of redemption
For all that was taken,
For this is a time
When all will be shaken.

He is aligning
All things to His plan
Through the process
Of His winnowing fan;

Shaking asunder
The enemy's ties,
It is time for the opening
Of spiritual eyes;

Understanding revealed
For these last days,
Everything that has breath
Will give Him praise.

This is the time,
This is the hour
To have all restored
By the Father's power.

Eternal Function
(The Effectual Calling into Destiny)

I received a vision during a worship gathering shortly after Rosh Hashanah 5777, the year of the Ruling Sword (September 2016). What I saw was so profound in relation to the Hebraic year and the timings of God. With all spiritual things, there are times and seasons in our personal journey where eternal truths are revealed and relevant. Yet in the prophetic timeline of God, there are key times that are "kairos" moments versus "chronos" moments. From the Greek language (New Testament writing), "chronos" is chronological time, "Kairos" means "head", as in things coming to a head; a divine appointment or season.

In the vision, I was in a field that was filled with golden grain, as far as my eyes could see, glistening and moving gently in the breeze. The whole atmosphere was one of golden luminescence. In the distance was a throne, elevated upon a mountain. As I looked to the throne, Jesus left it and came to the field. He was both close to me yet far away, I could see him clearly, His eyes compelling me to come to Him, yet He was a ways off. He was clothed in robes of crimson and pure white. He looked upon me and I felt Him drawing me to come, yet I felt hesitancy. He took off His robes, and somehow they were compacted into a tight roll, because then with a powerful force, He unfurled them toward me and they became a path. As I felt the power of authority in the unfurling, the hesitancy left and I immediately ran to Him. In fact, the power of the release of the robes became a knowing in my own identity and it was immediate, no thoughts at all, all hesitancy gone. As I embraced Him, the robes reformed into a feathery, yet impenetrable, shield of iridescent purple around us and we became one and were spinning and rising into higher elevation.

I asked Holy Spirit about the vision, why crimson and white robes. He said that the crimson represented the shed blood of Christ and the white was purity. I represented the Bride. As we receive the full revelation of our identity and calling in the authority of His shed blood, and the purity of His life, we will become one in His authority. In that place of oneness, nothing of harm can enter. It is impenetrable, and we will rule from a higher place where He is.

The Lion of Judah Roars

Seeing others filled with wonder
As your power from heaven thunders.
Moving mountains, kingdoms shake
As the land, for you, we take.

There is no greater we can do
Than live our lives giving glory to you,
For all things in the earth are yours
Your eternal purpose is what endures.

As we move forward,
Our spirit soars
And the Lion of Judah roars,
Opening the everlasting doors.

Eternal Exhortation
(Go Again)

In the fall of 2016, there was a period where I felt dry and empty. Late fall is usually challenging for me spiritually, as the world gears up for Christmas and I struggle not to get caught in the trappings of busy-ness and overspending, losing sight of the meaning of the season. It is a busy time of multiple birthdays also, with one daughter and two grandchildren in November and December.

It is interesting to me, that organizing these writings after receiving such a strong word (The Effectual Calling into Authority), I entered into a dry time. This is something that I have seen as a pattern. Our faith is "tried" or proven, on the words that we receive. Now I *know* that, and have counseled others on that truth, in fact it is a key teaching in "Moses — Shocked in the Desert, Learning God's Ways So We Can Enter the Promised Land." However, when in a trial, I don't remember this truth. Afterwards I see it.
During this dry time, I sought the Lord for a word of encouragement. I heard, "a sound of abundance of rain."

In I Kings 18, Elijah told King Ahab that there was a sound of abundance of rain. Sound in the original language means a noise or a voice. This was a word from the Lord that Elijah had been waiting for, it signified the end of a period of drought. Three and a half years prior, Elijah had prophesied to King Ahab that there was a drought coming, because he and the people of Israel had ceased following the Lord.

One of the meanings of drought is sword. When the word of the Lord comes to divide, it is to cut off ungodliness and allow His Lordship to reign. The people of Israel had been under the sway of evil, following the false prophets of Baal. At the Lord's time, Elijah came to bring the other edge of the sword. This was the showdown between the Lord and Baal. God showed Himself to the people as the One True God and the prophets of Baal were destroyed. The people's hearts were restored to the Lord. During drought, the sword is doing the work of cutting out ungodliness so that the false in us (all the lies of the world, the flesh and the devil) can be "showed up" by God.

It is when our hearts are turned fully to the Lord that the fullness of His presence – His reign bringing His rain – comes again into our lives. When we hear a sound – the voice of the Lord telling us that there is the fulfillment of a prophetic promise at hand – we must continue in prayer and faith until we see the manifestation.

Elijah positioned himself in prayer, and sent his servant to go look toward the sea. His servant went and came back after seeing nothing. Elijah told him to go again seven more times, until he came back saying he saw a cloud the shape of a man's hand.

"Servant" in this verse means tumble, shake, as a lion's mane shakes when he roars! The root of the word "sea" also means to roar.

When we are going on in faith on God's word (a sound of abundance of rain), we have to shake off doubt and unbelief; we have to rouse up our faith and let the Lion of Judah – the Spirit of Christ within us – ROAR from the Spirit into the natural until the time of the completion of the word – seven times signifies that process.

Your voice is your servant. It is by speaking our voice in faith that we are sending our servant forth into the atmosphere of our circumstances, declaring that we believe God's word and will continue believing until we see the manifestation of that word.

Go again! What the Lord has said to you is true and will come forth. The enemy comes to bring doubt and fear, to cause you to speak forth words of doubt and deny your faith in what God has said! Deny the enemy any ground in you! Does it seem hopeless, based on your circumstances? Go again!

Your voice is your servant. Remember what the Lord has said; hear the sound of abundance of rain and rouse your faith! Send your words forth and declare the promises He has given you; bring them forth with the lion's roar until you see the cloud the shape of a man's hand. The hand represents power. God is waiting for us to agree with Him and use our words as seed. The rain will come to water the seed and bring it to fullness!

Is our God not a God who can perform what He has spoken? *"So shall my word be that goeth forth out of my mouth: it shall not return unto me void, but it shall accomplish that which I please, and it shall prosper in the thing whereto I sent it."* Isaiah 55:11 (KJV)

I hear a sound of abundance of rain! Go again! Rouse your faith and roar from your spirit into your circumstances until you see the power of the Lord in your life! This is a time of His appearing; the rain is coming! Let Him reign!

Eternal Encouragement
(A Season of Suddenlies)

Mid-December 2016, I heard the Lord say we are in a season of "suddenlies." The things we have been believing for, waiting for, praying for – the season is upon us for the fulfillment of those dreams.

Suddenly, health restored. Suddenly, prodigals come home. Suddenly, financial provision. Suddenly, relationships restored. Suddenly, open doors. Suddenly, light in dark places. For this is a season of light shining in the darkness, a season of miracles, a season of the alignment of natural with spiritual.

> *"And as he journeyed, he came near Damascus and suddenly there shined round about him a light from heaven:"* Acts 9:3 (KJV)

I hear the Lord saying that, **"Even as Saul was on his journey, doing what he thought was right for his life, the appointed time and my sure purpose for his life had arrived, so it shall be with you. You have been on your journey, being faithful in the things set before you, and now the appointed time is upon you for my purposes to be established. My light will come and illuminate every dark place where you have given up hope. My light will come and show you the next step to take. My light will come suddenly, and you will know, even as Saul knew, that I am the Lord of Glory. For My Glory will come to you and you will come to my Glory and you will become my Glory in the earth for such a time as this. For Glory will cover the earth through My people walking in My ways. My ways are higher than your ways, and my thoughts than your thoughts. You are wearied with many plans, for a man's mind plans his ways. Yet My suddenly is upon you.**

My suddenly will bring My ways, and My path will open for you, and you will know Me in a way you have not known, and I will take you upon a path that you have not known. You have been trying to think your way through and into a place where you have not been and you know not the way, but as I told you in My Word, I am preparing a place for you. My kingdom is at hand. I am preparing the place for you and I alone will lead you to it. The

"place" is not a physical place, it is a place in the Spirit where moment by moment I will make Myself known to you and lead you in the way you should go.

Do not be afraid, but trust in Me. Have I not always been faithful? Have I not always provided? This is a time of remembering that I AM faithful. Yet do not look for me in the way you have seen me in the past. I AM always bringing you forward and upward into My glory, it will not look the same as before. Suddenly, the light will shine. Suddenly, your provision will come. Suddenly, you will be astonished and amazed. Though you trust me, your trust has been in my faithfulness as seen by my past provision in a present moment. Now I will shine light onto the road of your future, and your eyes will be opened to the limitless realms of My eternal glory in ways you have not known."

This is a season of miracles. This is a rare time, when Hanukah and Christmas coincide. This is a season of light shining in the darkness, a unity of people celebrating God's faithfulness and goodness, His miraculous provision for our present and hope for our future. This is a season of expectation and hope. Prepare to be astonished at the sudden appearing of the light of His Glory in your life.

Eternal Rest in Waiting for the Birth of Promises

There is always a waiting period, waiting for the things God conceives in our spirit (through the Word, a prophecy, or a dream or vision and the subsequent revelation of meaning). During a waiting period in late 2016, I had been reading the first two chapters of Luke and the Holy Spirit had been highlighting Simeon. When Jesus was brought to the temple for circumcision, Simeon was led there also by the Holy Spirit and immediately recognized that Jesus was the Christ, the Anointed One, the One who was the consolation of Israel and a light to the Gentiles. Simeon had been waiting. Why? Not just because of the ancient prophesies that all of Israel was awaiting the fulfillment of, but because the Holy Spirit had told him that he would see the Messiah before he died. He was waiting in expectation for the fulfillment of that promise, trusting that God is faithful to His word. The Holy Spirit began to speak to me about my habit of worrying.

The next morning as I lay in bed, awake but not ready to get up yet, I noticed that the longer I lay there the more my mind went into worry. I realized I was filling the space of waiting with worrying. I took a step of determination to shake off worry, choosing to pray instead. Faith began to rise up and Holy Spirit brought to mind Mary's situation. I felt Holy Spirit prompt me to consider how Mary must have felt during her time of waiting and what she did.

I knew that during the waiting time there had to be some kind of doubts and fears trying to take hold, as the devil certainly wouldn't have left her alone. Also, she lived in a culture where it was shameful to be pregnant outside of marriage, let alone saying the Holy Spirit was the one who impregnated her! They didn't have pregnancy tests back then, so I am certain there were at least a few weeks of choosing between wonder and worry. Plus, in any pregnancy, there are always things to worry about, or stay in wonder over the miracle of creation and birth! Not that I, or any of us are Mary, carrying the only begotten Son, but we are all carrying some Word of God that the Father desires to see birthed through us.

As I pondered this, I felt Holy Spirit prompting me to notice the similarities and differences between Mary and Zacharias in the book of Luke.

In Luke Chapter 1, the angel Gabriel appeared to Mary and told her that she was highly favored, that the Lord was with her and that she was blessed among women. Mary was troubled at his saying, and "cast in her mind" what manner of salutation this should be. And the angel repeated that she had found favor with God and not to fear.

She was troubled and "cast" in her mind. "Cast" in the Greek language (New Testament writing) means to reckon thoroughly, to deliberate (by reflection or discussion), to consider, dispute and reason. It's okay to deliberate about something, to dispute in our minds and try to understand. After all, an angel appeared and told her she was highly favored, blessed among women, but didn't say why that was so. Yet I know from my experience that reasoning usually brings fear, and this must have been the case with Mary because the angel told her not to fear as she was reasoning in her mind.

Zacharias had also been visited by the angel Gabriel, and what happened in his situation? He was afraid. The angel also told him not to fear, explaining that he came in response to the prayers of Zacharias for a child. The angel then expounded the prophetic fulfillment that would occur through this child whose name would be John (Luke 1:13-17). Zacharias had been praying for this, yet didn't believe it when it was told him that it would happen, because of natural reasoning — (Whereby shall I know this? for I am an old man and my wife well stricken in years). He was told that he would be dumb, unable to speak, until the fulfillment of God's word.

His child's conception was not an overshadowing of the Holy Spirit, a virgin birth. This was a birth from the union of Zacharias and his wife Elizabeth. I can only imagine how Elizabeth must have felt to be approached by a mute husband at her old age and then find she was pregnant, but she knew it was God's blessing and to take away her reproach at being barren. What happened when the baby was born? The people asked what the name would be and when Elizabeth said, "John," they were astonished. There had been no "John" in their lineage. It was the custom to use a family name. Zacharias beckoned for a tablet and wrote, "His name shall be John" and his mouth was opened.

When our hearts come into alignment with what God says, the chains of past pride, tradition and fear of man (Luke 1:57-66), will be broken and our tongue will be loosed. There may be chains on us not from the enemy per se, but because we have gone into agreement with the enemy — laughing and mocking (maybe in our hearts) at what God says — it's unbelief! The chains are on until we get into alignment with Truth.

Mary, after she was told what would happen, said, "How can this be, seeing I have not known a man?" Her heart was one of trusting, but in wonder, and the angel explained the prophecies that would be fulfilled through Jesus, then further added to her faith by telling her about her cousin, Elizabeth's pregnancy, that *"With God nothing shall be impossible."* Luke 1:37 (KJV) Mary's response? *"...Behold the handmaid of the Lord; be it unto me according to thy word...."* Luke 1:38 (KJV)

There are similarities with Zacharias and Mary; what are the differences? Zacharias had been praying for a child. Mary had not been praying for anything. Zacharias was a priest and well along in age, implying he would be a man of faith and know the prophecies, certainly aware of angels appearing as spokesmen of God. His response was unbelief and mockery in his heart. He had become hardened in his heart. It was a gracious act of God to render him dumb until such time of fulfillment of the word. The prophecies would be fulfilled, and the priest would not be speaking unbelief and faithless words in the process.

Mary responded with willingness to allow God to use her. Then came the waiting period. What did she do during that time? She went to Elizabeth. She went to one that the angel told her was also in process of a miracle unfolding, a manifestation of God's word. Mary chose to move into an environment of faith. Certainly, she had questions!

> *"Then said Mary unto the angel, How shall this be, seeing I know not a man?"* Luke 1:34 (KJV)

She was a virgin, pregnant with a child of the Holy Spirit!

I am not Mary, and what God has shown me is not the miracle of a savior being born through me. Yet I am carrying great and precious promises that

He has given me, things that I have not experienced before and I have no idea how this can be, how He will do it!

God is so good; He sends confirming words through others to encourage us if we stay in faith during the waiting process.

> *"And there were in the same country shepherds abiding in the field, keeping watch over their flock by night. And, lo, the angel of the Lord came upon them, and the glory of the Lord shone round about them: and they were sore afraid. And the angel said unto them, Fear not: for, behold, I bring you good tidings of great joy, which shall be to all people. For unto you is born this day in the city of David a Saviour, which is Christ the Lord. And this shall be a sign unto you; Ye shall find the babe wrapped in swaddling clothes, lying in a manger.*
>
> *And suddenly there was with the angel a multitude of the heavenly host praising God, and saying, Glory to God in the highest, and on earth peace, good will toward men. And it came to pass, as the angels were gone away from them into heaven, the shepherds said one to another, Let us now go even unto Bethlehem, and see this thing which is come to pass, which the Lord hath made known unto us.*
> *And they came with haste, and found Mary, and Joseph, and the babe lying in a manger. And when they had seen it, they made known abroad the saying which was told them concerning this child. And all they that heard it wondered at those things which were told them by the shepherds.*
> *But Mary kept all these things, and pondered them in her heart. And the shepherds returned, glorifying and praising God for all the things that they had heard and seen, as it was told unto them."* Luke 2:8-20 (KJV)

Mary received confirmation on what was told her by the angel as to the purpose of Jesus. She pondered all these things – thinking on them, considering all that had occurred and seeing the hand of God in her life as the path unfolded.

Our paths are continuing to unfold as we wait for the fulfillment of His promises. I know what the proper response is for the fulfillment of His promises – faith! Faith, believing, is a matter of our heart towards God. Our hearts direct our seeing, our perceiving, and out of the abundance of our hearts, our mouths speak. Be it unto me according to your Word, Lord.

> *"For the eyes of the Lord run to and fro throughout the whole earth, to shew himself strong in the behalf of them whose heart is perfect toward him..."* I Chronicles 16:9 (KJV)

We serve an awesome God, an amazing, magnificent Creator who loves to show off. We are to wonder, but not worry. He is omnipotent, faithful and true; His eyes are on you! Be filled with wonder that He loves us so greatly and desires to use us for His great purposes in the earth! Rest in the knowledge that He that has begun a good work in you will be faithful to complete it! (Philippians 1:6) Let it be done unto us in accordance with His word!

Eternal Reality
(Continual Expansion)

On December 24, 2016 (Christmas Eve/beginning of Hanukkah), I was relaxing in the living room with a fire in the fireplace. It was a very cold, rainy and windy day. My gaze turned toward the back yard, as it often does, as we had a beautiful elm tree that was central to our garden. I noticed that the lowest branches seemed lower over the fence line than they had been, and I felt fear grip my heart. I went outside to investigate further, hoping that I was mistaken.

I know my yard - every tree, every flower, the way the light shifts shadows at different times of day, the length of the branches as the tips stretch towards the canyon. One of the first things I do each day, before the dawn breaks and the first birdsong is uttered, is go onto my porch and cry out to God. I stand there in the dark and declare that Jesus Christ is Lord, to the Glory of God the Father. I know my tree.

My scrutiny continued, this time estimating the distance between the top of the tree and our awning. To my shock, the tree had listed toward the canyon by at least two feet. I went into the yard and upon closer examination, saw that the point where the trunk meets the base of the tree in the ground had a large crack. In addition, a foot away, there was a gap in the soil that was parallel to the tree's base and I could see a separation where the tree was being uprooted by the wind.

I called the manager of our park and she called the tree service. Christmas Eve!!! He called me and told me it would be an hour. By the time he got here, the tree was another two feet towards the canyon. He trimmed off much of the weight on the canyon side, so that it wouldn't topple over and take out the fence, and it shifted back substantially. It was very weak at the base, though, and more rain and wind was forecast for later in the week. He advised that the tree would most likely have to be removed. I was heartbroken. I was thankful that he and his helper were willing to come out on Christmas Eve! I spent much of Christmas despondent and teary. I loved this tree; it was one of the reasons we chose this location. Our tree brought so much shade in the summer; birds of many varieties would come for seeds in the fall and shelter year-round. The tree brought privacy to our home and beauty of dappled sunlight to our yard. I was heartbroken. "Why would you let this happen, God?"

Over the next few days, I became adjusted to the reality that the tree would be removed. I knew that I would always be wondering and fearing when rain or wind were forecast, and the reality of rot setting into the crack was real. I was reminded of my prayers, that everything God had not planted to be uprooted, and all that He plants to remain. I couldn't make sense of it.

The day came too soon. Little by little the branches were removed until all that remained was a small stump. It looked like devastation had come to my yard. In addition, I wasn't feeling well physically and there were things going on in my family that were causing emotional upheaval as well. I was feeling a great deal of self-pity and trying to make sense of this loss. I was in prayer constantly, but the heaviness of loss and pain was so real that I wasn't hearing anything. I sensed a great heaviness from the tree-trimmer as well, and began talking to him. He was in a lot of pain in his knees. I asked if I could pray for him and he was very thankful. His countenance changed and became much lighter as he received a touch from the Lord. I was thankful that some good came from this event, yet was still very disheartened personally.

Knowing this is a season of light, I began searching light verses. I heard the Lord say, "The entrance of my Word brings light." I heard that in my spirit and it resonated throughout my being. Our home was filled with light, so much light, from the open expanse of unhindered light from the eastern sky. I sat on the porch and watched the clouds gather and recede, the changing patterns of brightness and colors as they shifted and reformed throughout the day. I could see so much more of the skyline and of the canyon. I heard the Lord say, "I am expanding your vision, your perception, and your horizons. This is the beginning of a new day when the things that were hidden will be revealed, and what was obscure will become clear."

New Year's morning I sat on my porch pre-dawn and sought the Lord. As I was seeking, praying and declaring His Lordship, a green meteor appeared from the east in the distance and I watched as it drew across the expanse of sky over my head and to the west. I was amazed. It was the first I had ever seen, and would not have been able to see it with the tree in place! I heard the

Lord say, "This is the first of what will be many supernatural occurrences. You will see and hear things that you have never before seen or heard. I am expanding your horizons, your perception, and your seeing and hearing, and you will be amazed."

We ministered at our convalescent home morning service a few hours later. Two people received healing. In the afternoon service, which is a very small group, we had a very intimate time of fellowship and were sweetly serving one another. It was so sweet that we all stayed way beyond our normal time.

God is good, and He is doing new things. This is a season of expansion and new beginnings, a season of increase in hearing and seeing, an increase in the move of God in our lives. Know that He is good, and that He has a reason for everything that occurs in our lives as He shifts the old to make room for the new.

The months subsequent to receiving this word, came a time of discouragement. Once again, I didn't notice the pattern at the time, nor did I recollect the "Expansion" word. Only in the organizing of the sections of this book did I see the pattern.

Eternal Strategies
(This is not a Set Back, it's a Set Up)

Once again, after receiving a strong word (Expansion), I entered into a period of discouragement, due to many occurrences of "problems" in my life over the last months that had to be dealt with — financial, career, family, illness — all seeming to indicate attacks by the enemy leading to setback and in direct conflict with words of promise I have heard from Him and been standing on. It was a real battle. I had been hearing these words, "Maybe God didn't really say all those things to me; maybe I imagined it; maybe I misheard or misinterpreted what I saw and heard." One morning during a time of desperately seeking a word from the Lord, I heard Him say, **"This is not a setback, it's a set up."**

He told me to go back to what He told me six-week prior during a consecrated time of seeking; I needed to read it again! This is what He had said previously:

"This is a time of expansion of horizons. Many things will be changing as I make way for the new. Many things will be uprooted and eliminated that in the previous season brought you great enjoyment, but in this season they would be a hindrance to your vision and perception. You must be ready, in the natural and in the spirit, to know that I am sovereign and that "this thing is from me."

> *"Thus saith the LORD, Ye shall not go up, nor fight against your brethren the children of Israel: return every man to his house; for this thing is from me. They hearkened therefore to the word of the LORD, and returned to depart, according to the word of the LORD."* I Kings 12:24 (KJV)

"Many events will surprise and even shock you as the shifting continues. I am moving hindrances out of the way for my work to be done. What was a blessing in the days before, will keep you from my best in the days to come. You may experience feelings of loss and pain. Do not let attachments to transient, temporal blessings bring a hardening to your heart towards me, or

an offence causing you to stumble. I am the Lord. There is no other, and I am a jealous lover. Know that I am good, always, and trust me even when you don't understand my ways.

> For there is coming a time in the days ahead
> When things may happen to fill you with dread.
> Turn your eyes to me, look ahead.
> Eyes single, focused on me, instead.
> It will be as I have said.
> I uproot and I tear down
> Structures and mindsets of others' renown.
> The day is coming and is today.
> Look again, seek and pray.
> Have I not said I will show you the way?"

I was hearing and seeing an arrow pulled back to go farther. I was reminded of a word that Chuck Pierce had recently written about arrows — that the Lord sometimes pulls us back so that we can go farther, and hit the mark. What I heard in my spirit is that I (and many others) are in a place of tension where the archer is pulling back on the bow as it is being readied to catapult the arrow to its intended mark. As I meditated on these things, I heard the Lord say,

"The bow is pulled back so that the arrow can go forward with greater force. While pulled back, you will feel the tension, at times it will be intense. I am using the place of tension to cause you to seek Me and to examine your heart once again, as we enter this time of Purim, a time of purification. In order to "hit the mark" in the spirit realm, there must be a fullness of My Spirit to overpower and overcome the forces of darkness, to take down the enemy where he currently has the land. You are being readied, set to go forward in the power of My Spirit. You cannot allow evil thoughts of Me — doubting my purpose and plans, i.e. "Did God really say?" during this time.

"Therefore thus says the Lord [to Jeremiah]: If you return [and give up this mistaken tone of distrust and despair], then I will give you again a settled place of quiet and safety, and you will be My minister; and if you separate the precious from the vile [cleansing your own heart from unworthy and unwarranted suspicions concerning God's faithfulness], you shall be My mouthpiece..." Jeremiah 15:19 (AMPC)

You must enter with a Caleb spirit — fully believing I AM with you and I AM who I said I AM and I AM fully capable of performing all that I have promised.

What seems a setback is actually a set up

To position you and ready you

To carry more of my presence,

To take up residence

In places the enemy has had precedence.

Be alert, be ready,

Allow no hesitance.

I AM and my ways reveal my greatness

And excellence."

For those in a place of discouragement, *take* courage! It is not a set*back;* it is a set *up!* You are being set up by the Lord and He is faithful to do what He has promised!

Eternal Process
(Divine Tuning)

In early April 2017, during a time of prophetic worship, I had a vision where the Lord showed me that we are in a time of divine tuning – being tuned to His voice.

I saw the earth and above the earth was a very large metal tuning fork, with three tines. I asked the Lord why three tines, and He said it was Father, Son and Holy Spirit working together to bring creation into alignment with their divine purpose. The three bear witness (1 John 5:7) and agree. This is what I heard:

"This is a time that my people are being brought into tune with My voice. There are many other voices clamoring for your attention, designed to bring you into agreement with the enemy's purpose. You are being fine-tuned to hear and follow only My voice, the voice of the Bridegroom, the Eternal Voice.

There will come a time when the sky will split with a great sound and all things created in My Son will be brought together in One, but for now those who have ears to hear and eyes to see, are feeling the pull of My Divine Tuning Fork. For it is as a magnet drawing you into alignment with My purposes. Everything not of Me is being repelled to be removed. My fork will sift, digging deep to divide asunder all that is not of and for My purposes. Everything that is hindering the hearing of My voice will be removed.

Do not be deceived, there are many voices that are not True. There is an element of truth that is intended to draw you away, but it is a perversion of Truth and will take you on a different path. The Three-in-One must all bear witness. Do not be deceived. There is a pure voice, a pure sound, and you must exercise all your senses to discern. For didn't I say to you that there would be false prophets and false apostles among you, even tares among the wheat. They are doing a work, but it is not of Mine. Be discerning and recognize the tension that you feel is the pulling toward My Kingdom.

You are being fine-tuned to be in complete alignment with My Voice. Be alert and watchful. Listen for the True Sound. Many other sounds will cause an excitement and a desire to follow after and see. The three must agree. Father, Son and Spirit, One in the three, and on the earth, the water, the spirit and the blood all agree. Hear only Me, hear only Me."

"Who is he that overcometh the world, but he that believeth that Jesus is the Son of God? This is he that came by water and blood, even Jesus Christ; not by water only, but by water and blood. And it is the Spirit that beareth witness, because the Spirit is truth. For there are three that bear record in heaven, the Father, the Word, and the Holy Ghost: and these three are one. And there are three that bear witness in earth, the spirit, and the water, and the blood: and these three agree in one."   I John 5:5-8 (KJV)

Eternal Birthing

(You are crowing ~ don't stop ~ Keep your eyes on the prize!)

Mid-April 2017, I was hearing three things repeatedly – "Keep your eyes on the prize," "Birth" and Crown." I had been seeking the Lord about these things and what I heard is that we are in a time where the fullness of Christ in us is coming forth. Even as in the birthing process when the baby is crowning, it is time to push and keep pushing until the child comes forth from the womb.

Many are wanting to quit, and the enemy is whispering words of doubt and discouragement. This is not a time to pull back, but a time to press forth for the prize of the high calling of Christ Jesus in you!

The season was the beginning of months in the Hebrew; a time of having passed over and entering the land of promise. The root of the word month means rebirth, renew, rebuilding. This is the time when new things come forth. They are not sudden, but have been in process for some time. It is not time to quit.

When you are in a race, your body gets tired and you want to give up just before getting to the finish line. The Apostle Paul tells us what to do:

> "I press toward the mark for the **prize** of the high calling of God in Christ Jesus." Philippians 3:14 (KJV)

Why? To receive the crown!

> "Behold, I come quickly: hold that fast which thou hast, that no man take thy crown. Him that overcometh will I make a pillar in the temple of my God, and he shall go no more out: and I will write upon him the name of my God, and the name of the city of my God, which is new Jerusalem, which cometh down out of heaven from my God: and I will write upon him my new name." Revelation 3:11-12 (KJV)

"For Zion's sake will I not hold my peace, and for Jerusalem's sake I will not rest, until the righteousness thereof go forth as brightness, and the salvation thereof as a lamp that burneth. And the Gentiles shall see thy righteousness, and all kings thy glory: and thou shalt be called by a new name, which the mouth of the Lord shall name. Thou shalt also be a crown of glory in the hand of the Lord, and a royal diadem in the hand of thy God." Isaiah 62:1-3 (KJV)

In the eternal realms of God, there is no time, but He uses time to bring us from season to season. In a season of new beginnings, it is time to birth forth what He has begun in us. This is the time, this is the hour, for the Church to come forth in power! Hold fast, stay the ground you have taken. Push forth and bring to completion what He has conceived in you – His life!

I hear Him say – **"Keep your focus high, look to Me, look to Me. Do not let your sight grow dim; look to Me, look to Me. Keep your eyes on the prize, the time is nigh to realize, the old has come to its demise. It's time for the Church to arise; keep your eyes on the prize!"**

Again, in the process of organizing the sections of this book, I was surprised. In December, I was hearing about Mary and the conflict she must have felt during her pregnancy. Now receiving a word about birthing! The timing of God and how He reveals things to those who have eyes to see and ears to hear is amazing!

Eternal Direction
(Keep moving forward!)

In late April 2017, I heard the following:

There has been a shift; it's time to move forward. I hear the Lord say, **"As you have prayed and sought my face, I declare to you that NOW is the acceptable time, now is the season to move forward. The winds of change are blowing, listen and you will see which way to be going. I am opening doors that have heretofore been closed, you thought it was your foes, but I am unlocking bounty overflows. NOW is the time.**

You do not have to strive, the tomb of dead dreams has now come alive. Provision will come from unexpected places and unfamiliar faces. You will see, you will see, as the treasures of heaven come only from Me. My ways are not the ways of the world. As I open my hands, glory unfurls and makes its way to fulfill my plans. My ways are not as the ways of man. You have tried and pressed, you have done all you can, and now you will see my Divine Plan. It is not for naught; all the tears and the prayers, they have all ascended the heavenly stairs.

Now is the time, it has begun. Take hold of the vision and in the Spirit run. For this is not a natural thing, not a carousel's brass ring. My ways, I say, are higher than yours; I open and shut everlasting doors. Keep your faith high, keep your eyes on Me, you will see, you will see; what I AM has said, it is now and will be."

> *"Thus saith the LORD, In an acceptable time have I heard thee, and in a day of salvation have I helped thee: and I will preserve thee, and give thee for a covenant of the people, to establish the earth, to cause to inherit the desolate heritages;"*
> Isaiah 49:8 (KJV)

This word came when Kerry and I made the decision that now was the time for him to truly retire from the secular workplace. After making that decision, and him giving notice, two confirmations occurred. Another significant book order, and a request for us to expand our ministry at one of the facilities we currently serve. This is a key principle I have seen. We move forward in faith, sensing God directing but having to step out into the Jordan before it parts. After we make that move forward, He brings confirmation. In the natural, we hedge our bets. We analyze all the risks before stepping out. That is not faith. Faith is trusting Him and moving forward when we hear Him tell us to, even though in the natural we have no idea *how* it will all work out. He is a *super*natural God, Creator of the universe and all things are in His hands. He can direct others to provide exactly what we need, or provide the coin in the mouth of the fish and tell us to go fishing to get it! Matthew 17:24-27

Move forward!

> *"And the LORD said unto Moses, Wherefore criest thou unto me? speak unto the children of Israel, that they go forward:"* Exodus 14:15 (KJV)

Eternity Now
(Come Forth in My Glory)

We are continually moving forward into bringing the Eternal reality of the Kingdom of God into the earth. When I received this word from the Lord, I knew that this was to be the final chapter of my story. Being one in the glory and allowing His glory to be released through us on a daily basis is what brings clarity and fulfillment of purpose. Can you imagine if all of us poured out His glory? All the earth would soon be filled with His glory!

> *"But as truly as I live, all the earth shall be filled with the glory of the LORD."* Numbers 14:21 (KJV)

> *"It is the glory of God to conceal a matter, But the glory of kings is to search out a matter."* Proverbs 25:2 (NKJV)

I hear the Lord saying it is time to search out the glory within you! Even as the wise men saw the stars and searched out the Christ, the Spirit of God within you is constraining you to search within and draw out the glory. Search beneath the soulish realm, go deep until you hear the Holy utterance of the voice of the living God and let the roar of the Lion of the tribe of Judah release the sound that produces the glory in your circumstances.

Heaven is calling you forth. You are dissatisfied because you have fallen short of the glory! The Spirit of God, the life of Christ within you, is drawing you forth. This is the reason for your dissatisfaction. It isn't other people or your circumstances that are causing you grief. It is a holy dissatisfaction because you are falling short of the Glory of God that is within you.

> *"For all have sinned, and come short of the glory of God;"* (Romans 3:23 KJV)

We have all come *short* of the *glory*! (Romans 3:23) According to Strong's Concordance, sinning[3] can mean to be without a share in, and also to miss the mark. The root of the word means not to receive a part due or assigned to one or one's lot or destiny. Missing the fullness of our destiny! Jesus has paid the price; we have full access to our destiny, His life for ours! It is time to come forth into the fullness of Glory! He has prayed for us to be one with Him in the Glory; He has given us His glory! (John 17)

Heaven is calling and the earth is groaning. I hear the Lord say, "**Sons and daughters of the Most-High God come forth into the glory of the risen King. I have robed you from on high and filled you with joy unspeakable and full of glory (I Peter 1:8). Come forth, radiant ones, let Christ within you be seen and known. Fear has no place; it is but a stranger's face, and now, I say, I will erase and leave not even the smallest trace. All that is seen will be from My embrace. You are My imprint, My design. The world will see that you are Mine. Come forth, I say, let My glory shine.**"

I saw a vision of the Lion of the Tribe of Judah in a cage, panting, His majestic greatness pacing in the smallness of His surroundings. I could sense the fierceness of His desire increasing with each step, His power being held back by the bars of the cage.

I heard, "**The angels of the Lord Sabaoth (Lord of Hosts) are waiting, on alert, for the fullness of the sound of the army of the Living God to arise in the earth. The sound is building, take your place; come forth and roar! Do you hear the sound of heaven drawing? It is the eternal sound of your Holy calling!**"

I hear the Lord saying, "**Come forth, arrayed in My glory divine, robed with beauty, you are Mine. It is time to break through the cave of Adullam. You have hidden there long enough. Hear the sound of the wind in the mulberry trees.**"

I was confused, hearing the cave of Adullam along with the wind in the mulberry trees. My recollection was that they were two separate incidents. I felt Holy Spirit impress upon me to search it out. The cave of Adullam is where David hid with his band of distressed, indebted and discontented men (I Samuel 22). From these 400 came David's mighty army. After David was anointed King, the Philistines came against him and he went into the "hold," (2 Samuel 5:17) which Chronicles 11:15 indicates was the cave of Adullam. David sought the Lord and had victory. The Philistines re-gathered and David once again sought the Lord.

"Therefore David enquired again of God; and God said unto him, Go not up after them; turn away from them, and come upon them over against the mulberry trees. And it shall be, when thou shalt hear a sound of going in the tops of the mulberry trees, that then thou shalt go out to battle: for God is gone forth before thee to smite the host of the Philistines."
I Chronicles 14:14-15 (KJV)

Adullam means, "justice of the people." It was a town of the Canaanites allotted to Judah and lying in the lowlands. The root is Adlai – "justice of Jehovah." What I hear by the spirit is that it is time for the justice of God to be brought forth in the earth. It is time to come out of the caves of hiding, the caves of "lowland" thinking and renew our minds to the highest realms – the mind of Christ. The veil has been torn, we have access to all. Our "lowland" thinking is creating the bars of the cage holding back the glory of God from manifesting in our lives! We needed to be in the cave for a time of healing and building, but it is now time for His justice to be enacted in the earth.

According to Strong's Concordance, going[4] (the sound in the mulberry trees) means marching. The armies of the Living God, the Lord Sabaoth, are on high alert, waiting for the sound to come forth, and He will go before us and fight our enemies!

I hear the Lord say:

"The host of heaven is on alert. Come forth, sons and daughters in the earth. It is time for the new sound to be birthed. It will cause a vibration that will affect every tribe and nation, an eternal reverberation. Come forth in my glory, my host is at hand. It is time to go forth and subdue the land. The subduing is not a laying down under, subduing will come when My sound rises as thunder. All will see and all will know that I AM the Lord; let My glory flow.

The sound will arise and cause a vibration aligning every tribe and nation, the sound of eternal reverberation."

The Final Word

At some point an autobiography must come to an end. I feel that an exhortation to come forth in His glory is a great place to end the telling of my story. We who are His are always moving forward toward the High Calling of God in Christ Jesus. We will always be in transition, becoming more and more conformed to the likeness of Christ until we see Him face to face (2 Corinthians 3:18, I Corinthians 13:12, Romans 8:29).

Keep moving forward, wherever you are. You have read my story, the transition from confusion to clarity, from broken to whole, aimless to purposeful, the redemption and restoration of myself and my family, and God-honoring conclusions I have come to in my journey of faith as I have seen His hand move in my life. I will end with this:

God is good. Always. You were in Christ before the world was formed, and all things were created by Him and for Him. Without Him nothing can be. Your choice in this life is to receive Him into your heart. You are already in **His** heart, but He wants to come into **your** heart and redeem all that the enemy has stolen from you. He created you to have relationship with you, to be Your Father and for you to be in complete, unhindered fellowship with Him and have dominion in the earth, to restore the earth to the Glory that it had before satan was given reign through man's sin.

His plan is for you to be a partaker of His glory, to use your life to have others be reconciled to His love and purpose. We are created to bring Him glory, to live our lives to be to the praise of His Glory. He is good, and His purpose and plan for us is good.

He is the Alpha and Omega, the beginning and the end. Every knee will bow. Yours will be bowing eventually, and if you wait too long you will regret the years you have wasted and the opportunities that were presented to you.

Trust me. You have heard my story, I know. I tried all the other roads, and only One God is worthy of my love and admiration, no other worthy of spending my life on. He is Worthy and the riches of His Glory far surpass anything the world can offer.

Turn to Him

Turn to Him now while it is yet today,
And He will set you on the way
That leads to life and joy and peace;
Turn to Him, give full release

Of all that you are grasping for,
Enter the everlasting door.
The Father waits, He longs for you,
Let Him heal you through and through,

And see how He
Makes all things new.
You will find that He
Is Faithful and True.

IF THIS IS YOUR DESIRE, HERE IS A PRAYER FOR YOU TO SAY:

Father God, I come to you in hope that you can make all things new in my life. I have tried it my way and my life is a mess. It seems impossible, but I have heard or read others bearing witness that with You, nothing is impossible. I am ready to fully give you my heart and my life. Have your way. I trust your word that says if I believe that Jesus Christ died for my sins, and believe in my heart and confess with my mouth that He is risen from the dead, I can be saved. Your light has shone upon my heart and I now see the Truth and it has set me free, and I thank you. I give you my heart and my life and ask that You direct me in the way I should go. I trust you and thank you for your grace and mercy. In Jesus' name, I pray. Amen.

MAYBE, LIKE ME, YOU WERE ALREADY SAVED, BUT BACKSLID. YOU CAN PRAY THIS:

Father God, I am so sorry that I didn't trust you fully and wanted to try it my way. I see that I was deceived, for you are truly the only way — Jesus you are the Way, the Truth, and the Life — and I give my life to you. Forgive me my sins, Father, and cleanse me from all unrighteousness. I know you are faithful to your word, so I stand on that word and ask that you re-align me to Your purpose for my life. I pray for those I have hurt along the way, and ask that you forgive me and forgive those that have hurt me also. I trust you. I ask that you lead me in the way everlasting for Your Name's sake. In Jesus' name, I pray. Amen.

IF YOU ARE FEARFUL ABOUT THE FUTURE OF YOUR CHILDREN OR GRANDCHILDREN BECAUSE OF YOUR SINS OR THOSE IN THE GENERATIONS BEFORE YOU, STAND ON THESE PROMISES:

*If we confess our sins, he is faithful and just to forgive us our sins, and to **cleanse** us **from all** unrighteousness.* I John 1:9 (KJV)

And Jesus was made a curse for us, He has given us power to become the sons of God when we believe and are born of the Spirit, restored by adoption to the destiny God intended for us! (John I: 12-I3, paraphrased)

*Know therefore that the LORD thy God, he is God, the faithful God, which **keepeth covenant** and mercy with them that love him and keep his commandments to a thousand generations.* Deuteronomy 7:9 (KJV)

"And all thy children shall be taught of the LORD; and great shall be the peace of thy children." Isaiah 54:13 (KJV)

"But thus saith the LORD, Even the captives of the mighty shall be taken away, and the prey of the terrible shall be delivered: for I will contend with him that contendeth with thee, and I will save thy children." Isaiah 49:25 (KJV)

"Thus says the LORD: "Refrain your voice from weeping, And your eyes from tears; For your work shall be rewarded, says the LORD, And they shall come back from the land of the enemy. There is hope in your future, says the LORD, That your children shall come back to their own border." Jeremiah 31:16-17 (NKJV)
"So they said, "Believe on the Lord Jesus Christ, and you will be saved, you and your household." Acts 16:31 (NKJV)

"For the unbelieving husband is sanctified by the wife, and the unbelieving wife is sanctified by the husband: else were your children unclean; but now are they holy." I Corinthian 7:14 (KJV)

Our God is a God of covenant. Keep walking with the Lord and your faithfulness will be rewarded. He loves your children more than you do, and has a plan and purpose for their lives! He is the restorer of the breach, and the redeemer of our souls. He has paid the price, and we are His inheritance. God will see to it that Jesus receives all that He is due!

Jesus was made a curse for me, to take my curses upon Himself. His shed blood covers every sin I have committed and the sins of my lineage. I stand on that truth when the enemy whispers his lies to bring fear into my soul for my children and grandchildren. I declare those iniquitous roots are broken. The truth is that the sure mercies of David are mine, that I am in covenant with the Most-High God, and this extends to my future generations.

Prayerful Waiting

When I see sin rear its ugly head
I remind satan that the old man is dead;
No longer enslaved to my flesh or my soul
Christ took my sin so I can be whole.

Wholly living for Him alone,
He is King upon my heart's throne
And God Himself will make a way
For my loved ones also, as I pray.

He does not lie, His word is true
His covenant is sure; mercy will ensue
His purpose is good and His power is great;
I will trust Him as I wait,

Proclaiming His truth
And telling my story,
Determined that He will get
All the glory.

ENDNOTES

Strong's reference

1   James Strong, New Strong's Concordance of the Bible (Nashville: Thomas Nelson, 1995) s.v. obedience

2   Strong, s.v. glory.

3   Strong, s.v. sinning.

4   Strong, s.v. going.

Appendices

APPENDIX A

Becoming an Overcomer in the Daily Battle

Although the demonic voices ceased when I got saved, there were still daily choices that I had (and have) to make, and the many conflicting "voices" that contend for first place in my life. These "normal" voices that cause confusion for all of us I found most prevalent when the temptation to sin occurred. Other "voices" created conflict when there was a big decision to be made and I was afraid of making the wrong choice. The spirit of fear was a voice that paralyzed.

There was (and is) also the reality of being too busy to take time to be still and listen, to allow my mind to process all that is happening when my life is hectic. One of my favorite devotional books, *Springs in the Valley*, by Mrs. Charles E. Cowman, has a story of a missionary being led to a village by tribal people. He was hurrying them along, and after a few days they all sat down and refused to go any farther. He questioned them, and they replied, "We have to take time for our souls to catch up with our bodies." I have been in this training for some time. When I don't obey, "sickness" or some other affliction comes and I am forced to be still and listen. I am not saying God causes sickness, but if we are not in His will or correctly examining ourselves (I Corinthians 11:27-32) we are open to attack.

You may be thinking, "How in the world am I supposed to take hold of this when I am in a daily battle for peace?" You have to wage war in your personal life first. I am just trying to cast the vision so that you can see your purpose is much bigger, than just getting through day by day. Yet we have to do that.

Wherever you are in your walk of life, you have to wage war against the onslaught of negativity, even evil, thoughts that bombard us daily. Whether you are surrounded by it at home, or in the workplace, or it is "just" (not taken lightly) your personal thought life, you will have to be on guard. Why? To live a life that is victorious and fulfilling; to fulfill your calling and destiny in Christ. Do I need to bring it down to a more practical reality? If you want to be a good mom, a good dad, a good daughter or son, a good employee, a person who is highly regarded (especially to yourself), if you want internal peace… the right thoughts are critical!

So there we are, back to the battle…the battle is in our mind. There have been many books written on this subject. We have to tear down strongholds, high thoughts that are not what God says about us – they are lies of the devil. So how do we know which thoughts are true? Part of that is knowing what God says…reading His Word – the Bible. One of the biggest victories, and one of the most impactful in my life, came from getting into the Word daily.

IDENTIFY THE SOURCE OF THE VOICES

Whenever there is conflict in my mind, I try and identify the source. (See "A Helpful Tool" section for more information on how I do this in my life.) Of the voices that we hear, I believe there are three main sources – God, the devil and our own. The voice of the world system I include as the devil's voice, since he is prince of this world (Ephesians 2:2, 2 Corinthians 4:4, John 12:31, 14:30). Some say there are only two voices – God's and the devil's, and the only thoughts we have are one or the other.

Mark Twain is quoted as saying, "There is no such thing as a new idea. It is impossible. We simply take a lot of old ideas and put them into a sort of mental kaleidoscope. We give them a turn and they make new and curious combinations. We keep on turning and making new combinations indefinitely; but they are the same old pieces of colored glass that have been in use through all the ages."

I am including our own voices, (most of which are really imprints of other voices), but still one of the major sources. If you consider the multitude of voices and the influences of the voices (TV, internet, other people, etc.) it can be confusing to try and figure out how many "voices" there actually are.

So for the purposes of this section, I am saying that the source of the voices we hear on a daily basis are God, the devil and our own. If we consider our own, you probably notice there is a conflict (if you are a Christian). That is because we have the mind of the flesh, and the mind of Christ. The mind of the flesh is sense and reason without the Holy Spirit bringing His influence (Romans 8:5, AMPC). Jesus talks about this a lot – saying things like, "why do you reason in your minds" or, "take no thought." Obviously there is conflict in our thoughts.

One of the most compelling passages of scripture for me has been, *"Take every thought captive to the obedience of Christ."* 2 Corinthians 10:5 (KJV)

As I mentioned in an earlier section, according to the original text, obedience actually means attentive hearkening! Attentive hearkening; think about that! How can you attentively hearken to the voice of Christ? Well, first you have to be very still. You have to be at peace. When this scripture is making an impact on me, it is because I am bombarded with thoughts that are causing turmoil and confusion.

I used to think that this scripture meant I should start confessing the scriptures that combat the negative thoughts that were holding me captive, such as saying, "God has not given me a spirit of fear, but of power, love and a sound mind." Or, "I have the mind of Christ." Or, "God works all things to the good of those who love God and are called according to His purpose."

Now that I have read what the original language actually means, this is saying something much different and more significant to me. This is saying that to first, be still and know that He is God. Period. Be still. He is here with me. He has never left me, will never leave me, will never forsake me. I am His. Now, in that place, let me hear what the voice of the Spirit of Christ is saying to me right now. Not trying to call to mind things that may help if I confess them enough, (behavior modification), which is good and necessary; after all the Bible says, "think on these things, things that are pure and lovely..." We need to do that. But for me, the key has been "be still." That in itself is a challenge.

It is so necessary to hear what Holy Spirit has for me RIGHT NOW, because the rhema word of God is the word that will bring life; that will pierce and divide asunder the soul from the spirit. If I am in turmoil, it is my soul, not my spirit that is in ascendancy. For my soul is my mind, will and emotions.

If I am not at peace, it is my mind and my emotions that are swirling and agitating. My spirit needs to rise up and be in ascendancy, and by an act of my will I can make myself be still so that peace can come and I can hear the voice of God.

UNGODLY FILTERS

Another necessary step to clarity of hearing is recognizing we have filters. Our internal voice determines the base of our identity and reveals our <u>heart</u> issues — what we believe about ourselves, how we believe others view us, and how we believe God views us. Not what we "think" or "know" in our heads, i.e. what others tell us is true, or what we read is true, but what we believe deep down in the core of our being.

The external voices, i.e., what comes out of someone else's mouth — family, co-workers, friends, media, culture, and the world influence our internal voice daily. Think about how the advertisements we hear on TV, the images we see, even others' lives being promoted on social media create a negative voice as we compare ourselves to others.

We can't forget the silent (but loud in impact) voices in the spirit and mind — the mind of the flesh, filtered through our beliefs, and what we have listened to in the spirit - the devil and his demons or God by the Holy Spirit.

The reality is we are always hearing, always learning. We are processing what we see, hear, smell, touch and taste, and drawing conclusions. God has given each of us the ability to think, to grasp, to ascertain and learn so that we can grow. And there is a measure of faith He has given each of us (Romans 12:3).

What are we learning? What conclusions are we drawing? These conclusions are often based on reasoning through the filter of our beliefs that formed our identity, and these conclusions then form strongholds that can only be broken

by learning the Truth of our identity through the word of God and the Holy Spirit bearing witness.

In other words, if you had a parent who was very critical and belittling, and you were told continually, "that was stupid," you would be thinking you were stupid and filtering your experiences from that belief about yourself. As an example, if someone corrects you in a certain tone or with a certain look, you may immediately "hear" being called stupid or put down in some other way. This is your filter. Sometimes I do stupid things (like when I don't think about it first), but that doesn't mean I *am* stupid. When I make mistakes, it doesn't mean I *am* a mistake, nor does it mean I *always* make mistakes (i.e. the voice that says, "You never do anything right).

It reminds me of the truth that God loves the sinner but hates the sin. We often learn of God as a punitive, punishing God – that we are sinners and Jesus is our mediary. Yes, we have sinned and fallen short of the Glory of God. That is our sin. We have fallen short of the Glory that we were created for. However, when we confess our sins, God is quick to forgive and cleanse us from unrighteousness. We are made new again. Free to choose rightly! Free to believe we are created in His image! Free to trust Him and look to Him for guidance as a child would look to a good parent for direction! Free to live in His Glory!

God wants us whole and healed, our identity secure in Him, a relationship of intimacy and oneness, as was intended in the beginning before deception and sin entered in. He will continually bring to the surface those core identity issues – the lies – so we can bring them to Him, confess them and be healed – restored.

How does He bring them to the surface? Through relationships and our circumstances. Do you have poor self-image? It will manifest in your relationships. Do others treat you with disrespect and you allow it? Perhaps deep down you don't feel worthy of respect, or you believe that those "others", be it men, children, other groups, have "attitudes." Or perhaps it could be that *you* are disrespecting others and God is showing you *your* attitude by manifesting it through others around you.

God is sovereign and He has a plan. He engineers our circumstances in accordance with His plan. It may look like His plan is to harm you, but that's not true – it isn't over yet – and your idea of "harm" could be anything uncomfortable! He's trying to get you healed so you can walk in fullness and wholeness and fulfill His good plan in your life!

Much of our journey forward requires rigid self-examination in light of scripture. It isn't just memorizing, though that is important; the information in our *heads* has to get into our *hearts!* First we have to *see* what is in our heart and <u>hear</u> what God is saying through our circumstances.

Moses knew His ways, the Israelites knew His acts (Ps. 103:7). We first learn by His acts in our lives, then if we are obedient, our understanding becomes enlightened to His ways. Every step of obedience is a step of enlightenment. He doesn't illuminate until we take the step forward.

We want it all laid out ahead of time, to be able to see the next step, or the reason why. That's not God's ways, it is our trying to be God. Yet when we are obedient, He reveals things to us and we begin to understand by relationship. We don't give ourselves, our hearts, to another until we see by their acts that they are true. Don't we <u>all</u> want to be wanted, needed, desired for who we are, not for what we give? Not loved by "duty" or as "requirement" but seen as worthy of attention, others *wanting* to be with us? Talk is cheap. And so it is with God's heart — He doesn't show us everything until we prove ourselves true to Him.

APPENDIX B

Eternal Circle

I believe that when we are born, we are clearly hearing the voice of God, and seeing the presence of angels, aware of the spiritual reality that exists — eternity. I believe that we are sent by God to the earth, and in utero perhaps are still aware.

Very young babies often seem to be gazing into eternity, in wonderment at the presence of angels, or excited about the amazing sensory experience we have on this planet...dust motes shimmering in the light, caught in the air. They seem to be seeing angels singing over them with joy, hearing an unsung melody, content in the Presence.

Then we fill their lives with clutter of sight and sound, a cacophony of confusion. They adapt. Life happens. They forget, as we have forgotten.
Yet, at the appointed time, we hear an eternal truth that resonates deep within; a knowing, (Eph. 1:43, 11; 2:10; 3:11)

I believe it was Holy Spirit who revealed to me that I agreed to come and go through all that I have, to allow Christ to be formed in me in this world, for others to see and be brought home and to make known to the principalities and powers God's manifold wisdom (Eph. 3:10-11). The Bible says in Ephesians that we were in Christ before the world was formed, and that we are tri-part beings — spirit, soul and body. I believe that our spirit - one with Christ in eternity - agreed to come here and fulfill our assignment, then after we were born and immersed into the cold, harsh reality of the material world that is infused with sin because of the fall of man and the presence of the devil and his demons, we began the process of forgetting our eternal home.

> *"Jesus knowing that the Father had given all things into his hands, and that he was come from God, and went to God;"*
> John 13:3 (KJV)

I believe this because when I read about it and Holy Spirit revealed it to me, there was a *knowing* within, a deep truth that resonated within my being and it was as if the missing puzzle piece had been put into place. There have been subsequent experiences reinforcing my *knowing* and increasing revelation as I set my mind and heart to hear from Him and be obedient to His voice.

The hope that is in me has been born of the life of Christ Himself being formed in me, with the awareness of God's purpose. For Jesus is the Word of God made manifest, and His Life, through His Word, forms the nature and character of God within us, according to His purpose for our lives, which was ordained before the foundation of the world. There is a timing that only God Himself knows, and our purpose will come forth at that time.

His timing is not in the same system as ours, though. There is a culmination that occurs prior, and the mystery of this is that we do not know exactly how it works - our preparation by the Spirit Himself in our circumstances combined with our will and diligence to make the calling and election sure. I have seen that the reality is that, even when I think I have "missed" it, God already knows what choices I will make. When seen in the larger course of our lives, we can see that it all worked together for good. I can come down hard on myself with vain regrets (where the enemy tags in with his condemnation), but God knows that those places of "missing the mark" are the things that can push me forward as the spirit within me constrains me to keep pressing into the high calling of God upon my life.

> *"For if our heart condemn us, God is greater than our heart,*
> *and knoweth all things."* I John 3:20 (KJV)

There is the reality of all things already existing in the Spirit, and we must believe to enter in. Smith Wigglesworth is famous for saying, "Only believe," and he certainly walked in a much higher level of continual manifestation of Christ in his life than I do, or even most I have seen operating as ministers today. How much of our current reality is based on unbelief? Only God knows. Can we walk in newness of life in every situation or is there a process? It has looked in my life like a process.

There has been a breaking down of strongholds formed by circumstances and beliefs that were internalized as a child and young adult, determining that I will believe God's word over any thoughts and beliefs that I have that are in conflict to His Word. We are a new creature, old things are passed away and behold, He makes all things new. Yet in the day-to-day of life, at least for me, the flesh is still ever present with its desires, and my soul has deep areas where wounds occurred that God must heal.

The situations in my life, bring opportunity to identify wounds I have experienced and bring them to the feet of Christ. Only then can His life fill those places as I release the pain and His glory can take residence. It is Christ in us, the hope of glory. If we have areas of pain and wounds festering, it is not the glorious hope of His life manifesting, but our pain and the beliefs that keep the pain intact. We are releasing pain in the world, rather than His Glory.

> *"But rise, and stand upon thy feet: for I have appeared unto thee for this purpose, to make thee a minister and a witness both of these things which thou hast seen, and of those things in the which I will appear unto thee;"* Acts 26:16 (KJV)

> *"Whereof I was made a minister, according to the gift of the grace of God given unto me by the effectual working of his power."* (Ephesians 3:7)

> *"Whereof I am made a minister, according to the dispensation of God which is given to me for you, to fulfil the word of God; Even the mystery which hath been hid from ages and from generations, but now is made manifest to his saints: To whom God would make known what is the riches of the glory of this mystery among the Gentiles; which is Christ in you, the hope of glory: Whom we preach, warning every man, and teaching every man in all wisdom; that we may present every man perfect in Christ Jesus: Whereunto I also labour, striving according to his working, which worketh in me mightily."* (Col. 1:25-29)

> *"As every man hath received the gift, even so minister the same one to another, as good stewards of the manifold*

grace of God. If any man speak, let him speak as the oracles of God; if any man minister, let him do it as of the ability which God giveth: that God in all things may be glorified through Jesus Christ, to whom be praise and dominion for ever and ever. Amen." I Peter 4:10-11 (KJV)

"My little children, of whom I travail in birth again until Christ be formed in you," Galatians 4:19 (KJV)

There is a forming of His life that takes place in us. We minister through the ability that He gives us, the grace operating in and through us. His grace is both cause and effect. His grace causes His divine influence upon our heart to seek Him, and the effect of His grace in us causes His life to form. His grace causes us to desire to minister to others, and the effect of this grace is that Christ ministers to them through us. It is all a process of His effectual grace working in our lives, the praise of His Glory being the final result.

> **An Eternal God in us – His ETERNAL PRESENCE working through His ETERNAL PROCESS for His ETERNAL PURPOSE, resulting in His ETERNAL PRESENCE in our lives.**

About the Author

Alane Haynes is an apostolic and prophetic teacher and speaker, and has authored four books: "*Too Many Voices, My Journey from Confusion to Clarity;*" "*Moses – Shocked in the Desert, Learning God's Ways So We Can Enter the Promised Land;*" an accompanying *Study Guide;* and "*Called Unto His Presence,*" a compilation of Holy Spirit inspired poetry. Alane is a prophetic blogger and her writings have been featured on Spirit Fuel and Elijah List.

In 1981 the Lord Jesus Christ appeared to Alane and she was instantly saved, delivered and healed in body and mind. Her life is one of faith; she has seen countless miracles and answers to prayer in her life and others. Her passion is to see people restored to God's eternal design and purpose, walking in the fullness of their calling and living for the praise of His Glory.

Alane and her husband Kerry are apostolically aligned with Limitless Realms International Ministries in the San Diego Region. They founded and minister together through "Golden Vessels" and "Eternal Truth Now Ministry." Alane has been teaching and mentoring women since 2000, and is a leader in Women's Ministry at Rock Church San Diego. When they are not ministering, Alane and Kerry enjoy spending time with their children and grandchildren, and being outdoors enjoying the beauty of God's creation.

Website/blog: **www.alanehaynes.com**
Email: **eternaltruthnowministry@gmail.com**